Hindu Horizons:

Footsteps of Sanatan

Vipresh Dwivedi

DEDICATION

This book is dedicated to you—my fellow seekers, explorers, and enthusiasts of knowledge. It is for those who have embarked on the journey of discovery, eager to unravel the mysteries of Hinduism's global presence and its timeless wisdom.

In your hands, this book becomes more than just a collection of words; it becomes a gateway to understanding, a conduit for enlightenment, and a source of inspiration. Your curiosity, your passion, and your thirst for knowledge breathe life into these pages, infusing them with purpose and meaning.

As you navigate the narratives, delve into the histories, and ponder the insights within these chapters, may you find illumination and insight. May you discover new perspectives, uncover hidden truths, and forge connections that transcend time and space.

Your unwavering support, your endless curiosity, and your boundless enthusiasm fuel my own journey as a writer and a seeker of truth. It is to you, my cherished readers, that I offer this humble tribute—a token of gratitude for your companionship on this shared odyssey of exploration and discovery.

May the pages of this book serve as guides, companions, and companions on your own quests for understanding and enlightenment. And may the knowledge you glean from these pages enrich your lives, deepen your understanding, and inspire you to embark on even greater adventures of the mind and spirit.

ACKNOWLEDGEMENT

I would like to express my heartfelt gratitude to those who have guided, inspired, and supported me throughout the journey of writing this book. Their wisdom, encouragement, and unwavering belief in me have been invaluable, shaping the course of my exploration and discovery.

First and foremost, I extend my deepest appreciation to my beloved grandfather, whose stories of ancient wisdom and cultural heritage ignited my fascination with Hinduism. His tales, passed down through generations, served as the foundation upon which I built my understanding of this rich and vibrant tradition. His unwavering love and support have been a beacon of light illuminating my path.

I am also indebted to my teachers, mentors, and guides, whose guidance and encouragement have been instrumental in shaping my scholarly pursuits. Their passion for knowledge, their dedication to excellence, and their commitment to nurturing the intellect and spirit have left an indelible mark on my journey. I am eternally grateful for their wisdom, their patience, and their unwavering support.

To all those who have contributed to this endeavor—whether through scholarly insights, personal anecdotes, or moral support—thank you. Your contributions have enriched this work and made it possible to share the beauty and depth of Hinduism's global presence with the world.

In particular, I would like to acknowledge Sarita madam and Sudha madam, whose guidance and mentorship have been invaluable throughout the writing process.

Finally, to my family and friends, whose love, encouragement, and understanding have sustained me through the highs and lows of this endeavor, thank you. Your unwavering support has been a source of strength and inspiration, reminding me of the importance of community and connection in our shared pursuit of knowledge and understanding.

PROLOGUE

In the vast expanse of human history, amidst the tapestry of cultures and civilizations, there exists a thread that weaves its way through time and space—a thread that traces the contours of ancient wisdom, spiritual insight, and cultural heritage. This thread is Hinduism—a profound and multifaceted tradition that has left an indelible mark on the world stage.

From the sacred banks of the Ganges to the distant shores of Southeast Asia, from the majestic peaks of the Himalayas to the bustling streets of modern metropolises, the presence of Hinduism resonates far beyond the borders of its birthplace in the Indian subcontinent. Its teachings, rituals, and philosophies have permeated every aspect of life, shaping societies, influencing cultures, and inspiring millions across the globe.

In this book, we embark on a journey—a journey of exploration, discovery, and understanding. Through the pages that follow, we delve into the depths of history, archaeology, mythology, and spirituality to uncover the myriad ways in which

Hinduism has manifested itself outside the boundaries of modern-day India. From the temples of Angkor Wat to the shrines of Bali, from the manuscripts of ancient Persia to the syncretic traditions of East Africa, we trace the footsteps of Hinduism across continents and centuries.

But this is more than just a chronicle of historical events or archaeological discoveries. It is a testament to the enduring power of a tradition that has stood the test of time—a tradition that continues to inspire, challenge, and transform lives in the contemporary world. It is a celebration of diversity, resilience, and the universal quest for truth and enlightenment.

As we embark on this odyssey of exploration, let us open our minds and hearts to the rich tapestry of Hinduism's global journey. Let us honor the legacy of those who came before us and pave the way for future generations to continue the quest for knowledge, wisdom, and spiritual insight.

Welcome to the world of Hinduism beyond borders. Welcome to a journey that transcends time and space, illuminating the pathways of the human spirit and celebrating the universal quest for meaning and purpose.

Contents

PREFACE

In the kaleidoscope of human history, few cultural and spiritual traditions have left as profound a mark as Hinduism. While its epicenter resides in the sacred soil of India, the journey of Hinduism extends far beyond the geographical confines of the subcontinent. "Hindu Horizons" embarks on a compelling exploration, endeavoring to illuminate the global presence of Hinduism in ancient times—a presence that reached across distant lands, shaping the spiritual, cultural, and intellectual landscapes of various civilizations.

Recognizing Hinduism's Global Presence

To comprehend the global footprint of Hinduism, it is imperative to acknowledge the interconnectedness of ancient civilizations through trade routes, cultural exchanges, and intellectual dialogues. The roots of Hindu influence spread across regions that were once part of the expansive Silk Road, maritime trade routes, and the crossroads of Central Asia. This chapter sets the stage by delving into the historical context that allowed Hinduism to transcend geographical boundaries

The chapters that follow will unravel tales of symbiosis, tracing the roots of Hindu thought and practice in regions where diverse civilizations intersected. Through the lens of historical events, migrations, and cross-cultural engagements, we will witness the emergence of a truly global Hindu ethos that transcends national boundaries.

Exploring the Dynamics of Hindu Influence Beyond India

The aims and scope of "Hindu Horizons" are ambitious yet focused—a meticulous examination of the dynamics that propelled Hinduism beyond the confines of the Indian subcontinent. It is a journey that spans centuries, weaving together the threads of ancient civilizations and their shared cultural tapestry. Our exploration extends from the vibrant temples of Southeast Asia to the mystic heights of the Himalayas, from the trade routes of the Silk Road to the shores of East Africa. The scope is not limited to geographical expansion; it delves into linguistic influences, artistic expressions, and the enduring legacy of Hinduism in various corners of the globe.

The chapters within this exploration are designed to offer a comprehensive panorama, revealing the multifaceted nature of Hindu influence in diverse settings. Each chapter unfolds a unique aspect of this global tapestry, contributing to a holistic understanding of how Hinduism's impact reverberated across continents.

Unraveling Historical Narratives and Archaeological Evidence

The methodology employed in crafting "Hindu Horizons" is grounded in a meticulous examination of historical narratives and archaeological evidence. We embark on a scholarly journey, navigating through ancient texts, inscriptions, and artifacts to piece together the mosaic of Hinduism's global journey. By drawing upon the wealth of archaeological discoveries, we aim to unearth the material evidence that attests to the presence and influence of Hindu practices in regions far beyond India.

The exploration relies on a multidisciplinary approach, engaging with the works of historians, archaeologists, linguists, and cultural anthropologists. This collaborative effort seeks to bridge gaps in our understanding, providing a nuanced and well-rounded perspective on the dissemination and adaptation of Hindu traditions.

"Hindu Horizons" is an invitation to traverse the vast terrain of time and space, tracing the footprints of Hinduism as they echo through the annals of history. It is a journey that transcends borders, inviting readers to explore the rich tapestry of human civilization woven with the threads of Hindu influence. As we embark on this odyssey, the pages of this book unfold as a portal to the ancient past, illuminating the global horizons of one of the world's oldest and most resilient spiritual traditions.

Chapter 1: Seeds of Symbiosis

In the vast expanse of ancient history, Hinduism is eternal, as suggested by its original name "Sanatan," which means eternal. The term "Hindu" was later bestowed by different civilizations, inspired by the River Sindhu. For those residing near and beyond the river, the inhabitants were named Hindus. Hinduism is considered several lakhs of years old, with its roots reaching back to the beginning of the Big Bang. We encounter the emergence of written Vedic traditions around 1500 BCE, which were initially transmitted orally from generation to generation. This transmission was not limited to teachings alone; it also encompassed the nuances of pronunciation and pitch. The Vedas, a collection of sacred texts, became the foundation of early Hinduism, shaping its rituals, beliefs, and social structure.

Hinduism's roots extend deep into the soil of the Indian subcontinent, intertwining with the intricate traditions of the Harappan civilization, one of the world's earliest urban cultures. The archaeological remnants of the Harappan cities reveal a society with a sophisticated understanding of urban planning and intricate trade networks, hinting at a complex cosmology that laid the groundwork for the spiritual tapestry that would later become Hinduism.

However, it is within the sacred verses of the Vedas that we discover the earliest articulations of Hindu thought. The Vedic traditions, characterized by hymns, rituals, and philosophical reflections, form the cornerstone of Hinduism's spiritual philosophy. As these hymns were composed and recited over millennia, they absorbed the influences of indigenous cultures, gradually evolving into a dynamic and inclusive religious tradition.

Beyond the borders of the Indian subcontinent, the connection with nearby civilizations was integral to the development of Hinduism. Cultural exchanges with the ancient Persians, Central Asians, and other neighboring societies left an indelible mark on the evolving religious landscape. The synthesis of ideas and practices between the Vedic traditions and these neighboring civilizations enriched Hinduism, fostering a cosmopolitan ethos that embraced diversity.

In this exploration, we seek to unravel the

intricate tapestry of Hinduism's origin, acknowledging the interweaving of indigenous cultures, Vedic traditions, and the influences emanating from nearby civilizations. Through the lens of history and scholarship, we aim to discern the nuanced connections that gave rise to one of the world's oldest and most enduring spiritual traditions, a tradition that continues to shape the hearts and minds of millions.

Sanatan: Tracing the Origins of Hindu Thought

Sanatan, derived from the Sanskrit word "सनातन," translates to eternal or timeless. This term encapsulates the essence of Hinduism, suggesting a continuity that extends beyond the boundaries of time and space. In exploring the origins of Hindu thought, one must delve into the eternality embedded in the concept of Sanatan, a term not merely ascribed but earned through the profound resilience and adaptability of the religion.

Hinduism's designation as Sanatan is emblematic of its timeless nature, a quality inherent in the very fabric of its philosophy. The roots of Hinduism are intertwined with the dawn of cosmic creation itself, tracing back to the inception of the universe during the Big Bang. The cosmic hymns of the Rig Veda, one of the oldest sacred texts, echo the resonance of Hindu thought with the cosmic energies that birthed the universe. Thus, Hinduism is not merely a historical artifact but a living, breathing tradition that has withstood the ebb and flow of millennia.

The nomenclature "Hinduism" itself was a

label bestowed later in history, originating from the River Sindhu. It was neighboring civilizations, those residing near and beyond the River Sindhu, who named the people as Hindus. However, the essence of Hinduism, encapsulated in the term Sanatan, transcends geographical boundaries and is not confined to a specific region. Instead, it speaks to a universal truth, a perennial philosophy that finds expression in diverse cultural landscapes.

As we traverse the historical landscape, the emergence of written Vedic traditions around 1500 BCE marks a crucial juncture in the crystallization of Hindu thought. Prior to this epoch, the teachings were transmitted orally, a testament to the oral tradition's potency in preserving sacred knowledge. It was not a mere transfer of intellectual content but a comprehensive transmission that included the subtleties of pronunciation and pitch.

A unique method of preserving these nuances involved specific hand postures during chanting. The process ensured that the teachings and their intonations remained unaltered through generations. For high-pitched pronunciation, the arm was raised from the elbow; for medium pitch, it remained parallel to the ground, and for low pitch, it pointed downward. This meticulous approach reflects the commitment to maintaining the purity of the teachings, safeguarding them from distortion over the ages.

The Vedas, a compilation of these sacred texts, emerged as the foundation of early Hinduism. These ancient scriptures not only shaped the religious rituals but also laid the groundwork for the intricate web of beliefs and social structures within Hinduism. In essence, the term Sanatan encapsulates the timeless journey of Hindu thought, a journey that transcends the boundaries of historical epochs and geographical terrains, resonating with the eternal pulse of the cosmos.

Early Cultural Exchanges: Prehistoric Connections with Neighboring Civilizations

In the intricate tapestry of Hinduism's historical evolution unravels a narrative of profound intermingling between ancient cultures. Beyond the boundaries of what is now modern India, the roots of Hinduism extend into a web of connections with neighboring civilizations, creating a rich backdrop for the development of this timeless tradition.

Long before the establishment of formal borders and nation-states, ancient societies engaged in dynamic cultural exchanges that laid the groundwork for the synthesis of ideas and practices. The early connections between these civilizations served as the crucible for the nascent stages of Hindu thought, contributing to the diverse and inclusive nature that characterizes the religion.

One of the significant prehistoric connections lies in the cultural exchange between the inhabitants of the ancient Indus Valley Civilization and other contemporary societies. The remnants of the Harappan civilization, with its advanced urban planning and sophisticated trade networks, bear witness to a society that was intricately connected with its neighbors. The exchange of goods, ideas, and perhaps even spiritual concepts was facilitated through these networks, creating a fertile ground for the cross-pollination of cultures.

The confluence of ancient Indian cultures with those of Mesopotamia, Central Asia, and the Persian Gulf is another facet of these early exchanges. This crossroads of civilizations allowed for a vibrant exchange of not only material goods but also intellectual and spiritual concepts. It laid the groundwork for a cultural ecosystem where diverse traditions could coexist and influence one another.

In the realm of religion, these early exchanges sowed the seeds of Hindu cosmology and mythology. Shared symbols, motifs, and narratives found resonance across different cultures, shaping the pantheon of deities and the cosmogonic tales within Hinduism. The riverine symbolism, reverence for nature, and the concept of a cyclical cosmos were some elements that transcended regional boundaries, hinting at a shared cultural reservoir.

Furthermore, linguistic exchanges played a pivotal role in the development of Hindu thought. The interaction of languages in the ancient world, including the early forms of Sanskrit, paved the way for the rich tapestry of linguistic diversity within Hindu scriptures. This linguistic interplay not only facilitated communication but also allowed for the integration of diverse linguistic elements into the evolving religious discourse.

As we explore the early cultural exchanges that shaped Hinduism, it becomes evident that the roots of this ancient tradition are deeply entwined with the shared experiences of diverse civilizations. The chapter serves as a gateway to understanding how the fusion of ideas, beliefs, and practices during prehistoric times laid the foundation for the resilience and adaptability that defines Hinduism. It invites readers to envision a time when borders were porous, and cultural exchanges were the lifeblood of ancient societies, contributing to the rich and complex mosaic of Hindu thought.

Proto-Hindu Practices: Unveiling the Roots of Vedic Traditions

In the exploration of Hinduism's genesis, we endeavors to unearth the primordial seeds that blossomed into the intricate tapestry of Vedic thought. Delving into the obscured realms of ancient history, this chapter illuminates the early practices that laid the foundational stones of what we recognize today as Hinduism.

Early Cultural Milieu:

To comprehend the roots of Vedic traditions, one must immerse oneself in the cultural milieu that predates the formalization of Vedic scriptures. The term "Proto-Hindu" refers to the ancestral practices that form a bridge between the indigenous cultures of ancient India and the emergence of the Vedic worldview. These proto-Hindu practices reflect the nascent stages of a belief system that would evolve into the rich tapestry of Vedic thought.

Symbiosis with Nature:

At the core of proto-Hindu practices lies a

profound connection with the natural world. The reverence for nature, the cycles of seasons, and the symbiotic relationship between humans and the environment were integral facets of these early traditions. This harmonious coexistence with nature laid the groundwork for later Vedic concepts such as the sacredness of rivers, mountains, and the divine forces manifest in the elements.

Rituals and Ceremonies:

Proto-Hindu practices were imbued with rituals and ceremonies that sought to establish a communion with the divine forces believed to govern the cosmos. These early rites were deeply symbolic, echoing the cosmological understanding of the universe. As echoes of these rituals resonate in Vedic hymns and later Hindu scriptures, one can discern the embryonic forms of sacred ceremonies that would come to define Hindu religious observances.

Ancestral Veneration:

The veneration of ancestors and spirits played a pivotal role in proto-Hindu practices. The belief in a connection between the living and the deceased, with rituals designed to honor and seek guidance from ancestors, laid the groundwork for the intricate ancestor worship found in later Hinduism. This reverence for lineage underscored the importance of continuity and familial bonds within the evolving religious landscape.

Oral Tradition:

Before the advent of written scriptures, proto-Hindu practices relied on an oral tradition for the transmission of sacred knowledge. Elders and seers passed down hymns, chants, and rituals to successive generations, fostering a sense of communal identity and continuity. The transition from oral transmission to the recorded verses of the Vedas marks a crucial juncture in the formalization of Vedic traditions.

Symbolism and Cosmogony:

Proto-Hindu practices were laden with symbolic representations that conveyed intricate cosmogonic concepts. The use of symbols, metaphors, and ritualistic gestures formed the language through which early practitioners communicated with the divine. These symbolic elements laid the groundwork for the sophisticated cosmological and metaphysical ideas that permeate the Vedic texts.

In the exploration of proto-Hindu practices, one encounters the gestation period of a profound spiritual tradition. These early rituals and beliefs, rooted in the symbiosis with nature, reverence for ancestors, and a rich tapestry of symbols, set the stage for the flourishing of Vedic traditions. By unveiling these ancient roots, the chapter seeks to provide a nuanced understanding of the embryonic stages that heralded the emergence of Hinduism as a vibrant and enduring cultural phenomenon.

Chapter 2: The Silk Road Saga

Embarking on a historical odyssey, we unveil the riveting narrative of Hinduism's journey along the ancient Silk Road—a cultural and trade network that transcended geographical bounds, linking East and West. This odyssey along the Silk Road is a tale of crossroads, where Hinduism, with its profound philosophical roots and vibrant cultural expressions, became an integral participant in the dynamic exchange of ideas.

Woven into the very fabric of the Silk Road, Hindu thought found resonance amidst the bustling caravans and desert landscapes, leaving an indelible imprint on the civilizations it encountered. Beyond the mere trade of goods, the Silk Road became a corridor for the dissemination of spiritual wisdom, with Hinduism contributing to the rich tapestry of beliefs along the route.

This saga unfolds against the backdrop of bustling marketplaces, where merchants bartered not only silks and spices but also ideas and philosophies. The Silk Road, known for fostering cultural syncretism, bore witness to the confluence of diverse religious traditions, including Hinduism. Through this historical lens, we navigate the spiritual intersections, vibrant bazaars, and sacred landscapes that defined the transformative journey of Hinduism along the Silk Road—a journey that transcended borders and shaped the spiritual heritage of diverse civilizations.

Cultural Caravans: Hinduism Along the Ancient Silk Road

As we traverse the ancient Silk Road, we unravel a captivating chapter in the expansive tapestry of Hinduism's global journey. The Silk Road, a network of trade routes connecting the East and West, served not only as a thoroughfare for commodities but also as a conduit for the dissemination of profound philosophical ideas, including those rooted in Hinduism.

In the bustling marketplaces of Central Asia, where merchants engaged in the exchange of silks, spices, and precious goods, Hindu thought found an avenue to transcend geographical confines. The spiritual wisdom embedded in Hinduism, with its intricate cosmology, vibrant mythology, and philosophical depth, became an influential participant in the cultural exchange that characterized the Silk Road.

Temples and shrines dedicated to Hindu deities dotted the caravan routes, bearing witness to the assimilation of Hinduism into the diverse spiritual landscape of the Silk Road regions. As traders, pilgrims, and travelers traversed this ancient network, they carried not only material wealth but also the intangible wealth of ideas—ideas that would leave an enduring impact on the belief systems of regions far beyond the Indian subcontinent.

Hinduism's presence along the Silk Road was not a unidirectional dissemination but a dynamic exchange. As the spiritual currents of Hindu thought flowed along the Silk Road, they mingled with the diverse religious traditions encountered on this cosmopolitan highway. This cultural syncretism, evident in art, architecture, and religious practices, reflects the adaptive nature of Hinduism as it embraced and enriched the spiritual landscape of Central Asia.

The Silk Road thus became a corridor for the cross-fertilization of cultures, a meeting point where Hinduism engaged in a vibrant dialogue with Zoroastrianism, Buddhism, Taoism, and myriad other belief systems. The spiritual synapses formed along this ancient route endured, leaving an imprint on the collective memory of the Silk Road regions.

The Silk Road was not a single route but a network of interconnected trade routes that spanned vast regions of Asia, connecting the East to the West. The routes traversed a diverse range of landscapes, including deserts, mountains, and plains, and passed through numerous cities and regions. Here are some notable places along the Silk Road:

Chang'an (Xi'an), China: The eastern terminus of the Silk Road, where goods from the East were gathered for trade.

Dunhuang, China: A major oasis and cultural hub along the Silk Road, known for the Mogao Caves and Dunhuang manuscripts.

Taklamakan Desert, China: A vast desert that traders had to navigate on their journey along the northern branch of the Silk Road.

Samarkand, Uzbekistan: A key city on the Transoxianan route, famous for its architecture and as a center of cultural exchange.

Bukhara, Uzbekistan: Another important city in Central Asia, known for its role in commerce and intellectual pursuits.

Tashkent, Uzbekistan: The capital of modern Uzbekistan, which historically played a role in Silk Road trade.

Merv (Mary), Turkmenistan: A significant oasis city along the Silk Road, known for its wealth and cultural influence.

Persian Plateau (Iran): Various cities in Persia, including Isfahan and Shiraz, served as important trade hubs.

Baghdad, Iraq: A major center of trade, culture, and learning during the Islamic Golden Age.

Palmyra, Syria: An ancient city that served as a vital trading post along the Silk Road.

Antioch, Turkey: A crucial city connecting

the Silk Road to the Mediterranean Sea.

Byzantium (Constantinople/Istanbul), Turkey: A significant trading city that linked the Silk Road to Europe.

Trebizond (Trabzon), Turkey: A key port city on the Black Sea, facilitating trade with the Mediterranean.

Sogdian Cities (e.g., Samarkand, Bukhara), Central Asia: Thriving urban centers that played a crucial role in Silk Road trade.

Kashgar, China: An ancient oasis city and trading post on the westernmost end of the Silk Road.

Khotan (Hotan), China: An oasis city in the Tarim Basin, known for its production of jade and silk.

Kucha, China: A historic Buddhist center and trading hub along the northern branch of the Silk Road.

Karakorum, Mongolia: The ancient capital of the Mongol Empire, served as a meeting point for East and West.

Turpan, China: An important oasis town on the Silk Road, renowned for its grape cultivation and the Flaming Mountains.

Khiva, Uzbekistan: A UNESCO World Heritage site, Khiva was a key trading post on the Silk Road.

Otrar, Kazakhstan: A significant city along the Central Asian branch of the Silk Road, known for its role in the spread of Islam.

Tbilisi, Georgia: A crossroads of trade between the Silk Road and routes to the Caucasus and Europe.

Jerusalem, Israel: While not directly on the Silk Road, Jerusalem played a role in facilitating trade between East and West.

Tyre, Lebanon: An ancient Phoenician city that participated in maritime trade connected to the Silk Road.

Lhasa, Tibet: A high-altitude city that served as a hub for cultural and religious exchange between Tibet and the Silk Road.

Ayutthaya, Thailand: A historic city that engaged in trade with Silk Road merchants, influencing its cultural and economic development.

Samarqand, Tajikistan: Another Silk Road city that became a center of learning, culture, and trade.

Bishkek, Kyrgyzstan: The modern capital of Kyrgyzstan, situated along historical Silk Road routes.

Xinjiang, China: The entire region of Xinjiang served as a crucial crossroads, connecting East and West.

Tabriz, Iran: A historic city that thrived as a trading center and was known for its vibrant bazaars.

These examples highlight the immense geographical and cultural diversity along the Silk Road, illustrating the interconnectedness of civilizations across Asia, the Middle East, and Europe. The Silk Road's legacy is embedded in the histories of these cities, which collectively contributed to the rich tapestry of human exchange along this ancient network.

In tracing Hinduism along the ancient Silk Road, we uncover not just a historical trajectory but a narrative of cultural interconnectedness. The echoes of Hindu thought reverberate through the historical remnants of trade cities, the caravanserais, and the artistic expressions that dot the landscapes traversed by this ancient route. Through this exploration, we unearth the enduring legacy of Hinduism as a participant in the dynamic cultural exchange that defined the Silk Road—a legacy that transcends time and continues to resonate in the diverse spiritual traditions shaped by this historic journey.

Central Asian Confluence: Interactions with Zoroastrianism and Buddhism

In the intricate dance of religious evolution, the encounter between Hinduism and Buddhism along the Silk Road is a nuanced exploration of shared roots and distinctive transformations. Buddhism, born from the spiritual awakening of Siddhartha Gautama, a Hindu prince who would later become the Buddha, represents a unique facet of the complex relationship between these two traditions.

Buddhism's Hindu Origins:

Siddhartha Gautama, the historical Buddha, was indeed a Hindu prince born into the Shakya clan in ancient India. His quest for enlightenment was deeply rooted in the spiritual landscape of Hindu thought prevalent during his time. The foundational concepts of karma, samsara (cycle of birth and rebirth), and moksha (liberation from the cycle) were integral components of the Vedic and Upanishadic traditions, and it was within this milieu that Siddhartha's spiritual journey unfolded.

Synthesis of Ideas:

As Siddhartha embarked on his quest for truth, he engaged with and later transcended the prevailing Hindu philosophical concepts. The Four Noble Truths and the Eightfold Path, the cornerstones of Buddhist philosophy, emerged as transformative principles, distinct yet intricately woven with echoes of Hindu thought. The concept of nirvana, central to Buddhism, finds resonance with the Hindu quest for moksha, reflecting the shared aspiration for liberation from the cycle of existence.

Artistic and Ritual Confluence:

The artistic and ritual exchanges along the Silk Road further illuminated the interconnectedness between Hinduism and Buddhism. Temples and stupas, adorned with carvings and sculptures, reflected a syncretic blend of Hindu and Buddhist iconography. Deities from Hindu pantheons, such as Indra and Brahma, found their place within Buddhist artistic expressions, embodying the shared cultural heritage.

Cultural Evolution:

As Buddhism journeyed along the Silk Road, it engaged in a dynamic dialogue with diverse cultures, including Zoroastrianism and indigenous belief systems. The assimilation of local customs and the evolution of Buddhist rituals exemplify the adaptability inherent in the religious traditions born from the Indian subcontinent.

Legacy of Hindu-Buddhist Synthesis:

The interaction between Hinduism and Buddhism along the Silk Road left an enduring legacy, influencing not only the religious landscape but also the cultural, artistic, and philosophical dimensions of the regions traversed. The synthesis of ideas between these two traditions, rooted in a common cultural and spiritual ancestry, shaped the vibrant tapestry of beliefs that defined the civilizations flourishing along this ancient trade route.

In traversing the Silk Road, Buddhism stands as a testament to the profound interconnectedness of religious thought, where the roots of one tradition nourish the growth of another. The legacy of Siddhartha's journey from Hindu prince to Buddha becomes an integral part of the Silk Road narrative, reflecting the dynamism and adaptability inherent in the spiritual evolution that unfolded along these historic routes.

The interaction between Hinduism and Zoroastrianism along the ancient Silk Road is a captivating chapter in the history of cultural and religious exchanges. As these two ancient traditions encountered each other in the diverse landscapes of Central

Asia and Persia, a dynamic interchange of ideas, beliefs, and practices unfolded, leaving an indelible mark on both traditions.

Shared Cultural Landscape:

The Silk Road provided a thoroughfare for the exchange of goods, ideas, and religious concepts. Hinduism and Zoroastrianism, rooted in the ancient civilizations of the Indian subcontinent and Persia respectively, found themselves sharing a cultural landscape influenced by the cosmopolitan spirit of the Silk Road. This exchange fostered a cross-pollination of religious and cultural elements, enriching the tapestry of beliefs in the regions they intersected.

Cosmological Dialogues:

Both Hinduism and Zoroastrianism share fundamental cosmological themes such as the cosmic struggle between forces of good and evil. In Zoroastrianism, this is embodied in the perpetual battle between Ahura Mazda (the supreme god) and Angra Mainyu (the destructive force). Hinduism, with its diverse pantheon, also grapples with the cosmic balance of forces, personifying virtues and vices in its deities and narratives. This parallel in cosmological outlooks allowed for a certain degree of resonance and understanding between the two traditions.

Fire Worship and Rituals:

One notable point of interaction was in the realm of ritual practices. Zoroastrianism places significant emphasis on fire worship, considering fire as a symbol of purity and divinity. This practice found echoes in Hindu rituals where fire, known as Agni, is a central element in ceremonies such as

Yajnas and Havan. The shared reverence for fire as a sacred element facilitated a cultural and religious exchange that left imprints on both traditions.

Deity Assimilation:

The Silk Road served as a conduit for the assimilation of deities between Hinduism and Zoroastrianism. Hindu deities, such as Indra and Varuna, found their place in the cultural and religious milieu of Zoroastrian regions. Conversely, the Zoroastrian pantheon influenced certain pockets of Hinduism along the Silk Road. This assimilation highlights the adaptive nature of both traditions in response to the dynamic cultural interchange.

Artistic Synthesis:

Artistic expressions along the Silk Road also

bore witness to the interaction between Hinduism and Zoroastrianism. Temples and monuments reflected a fusion of iconography and artistic styles, embodying the synthesis of cultural and religious elements.

Cultural Tolerance and Coexistence:

The Silk Road was a melting pot of diverse cultures, fostering an environment of tolerance and coexistence. Hinduism and Zoroastrianism, along with other religious traditions, cohabited in certain regions, leading to a mosaic of beliefs that characterized the cultural landscape of the Silk Road.

In tracing the interactions between Hinduism and Zoroastrianism along the Silk Road, one discovers not only a convergence of religious concepts but also a testament to the adaptability and mutual enrichment that arises from cultural encounters. The legacy of this interaction endures in the historical remnants, artistic expressions, and shared cultural nuances that shaped the spiritual landscapes of the regions traversed by the Silk Road.

Transcending Boundaries: Hinduism's Influence on the Silk Road Trade Network

In the vast historical canvas of the Silk Road, Hinduism emerges not only as a profound spiritual tradition but also as a cultural and intellectual force that left an indelible imprint on the intricate tapestry of trade, commerce, and intellectual exchange. As caravans laden with goods traversed the vast landscapes connecting East and West,

Hinduism's influence resonated along the Silk Road in ways that transcended religious boundaries.

Cultural and Spiritual Exports:

Hinduism, with its rich philosophical heritage, artistic expressions, and cultural practices, became a cultural export that transcended the geographical confines of the Indian subcontinent. Temples dedicated to Hindu deities, adorned with intricate carvings and sculptures, stood as testaments to the vibrant spiritual and artistic traditions that found resonance along the Silk Road. These cultural exports not only reflected the diversity of Hindu beliefs but also contributed to the syncretic aesthetic that characterized Silk Road art and architecture.

Trade and Economic Hubs:

Cities and regions with a significant Hindu presence became vital nodes in the Silk Road trade network. Merchants from India, well-versed in trade practices and possessing a wealth of goods ranging from spices to textiles, played a crucial role in the economic dynamics of the Silk Road. Ports like Bharuch and Cambay became bustling centers facilitating maritime trade, connecting the Indian subcontinent to the broader Silk Road network.

Intellectual Exchange and Educational Centers:

Hinduism's influence extended beyond material goods; it contributed to the intellectual exchange that characterized the Silk Road. Educational centers in India, renowned for their scholarship in fields such as mathematics, astronomy, and philosophy, attracted scholars and seekers from distant lands. The transmission of scientific and philosophical knowledge along with religious texts became a significant facet of Hinduism's influence on the intellectual currents of the Silk Road.

Synthesis of Religious Ideas:

The Silk Road was a melting pot of diverse religious traditions, and Hinduism engaged in a dynamic dialogue with Buddhism, Zoroastrianism, Taoism, and other belief systems. This religious syncretism led to the assimilation of Hindu deities and concepts into the spiritual landscape of regions along the Silk Road. The exchange of religious ideas facilitated a sense of shared cultural heritage and spiritual syncretism.

Agricultural Innovations and Botanical Exchange:

Hindu agricultural practices and innovations in cultivation techniques influenced the agricultural landscape along the Silk Road. The introduction of new crops, such as spices and aromatic plants, brought about a botanical exchange that transformed the agricultural practices of the regions traversed by the Silk Road. The spice trade, in particular, became a hallmark of the economic exchanges facilitated by Hindu merchants.

Linguistic Influences:

The spread of Hindu cultural and religious practices along the Silk Road also left linguistic imprints. Sanskrit, the sacred language of Hindu scriptures, influenced the development of local languages in regions where Hinduism had a notable presence.

Inscriptions and texts in Sanskrit found their way into the linguistic mosaic of Silk Road cultures.

Cultural Synthesis in Art and Architecture:

Hindu artistic styles and architectural principles became integral components of the Silk Road's cultural landscape. Temples and monuments along the trade routes bore witness to the fusion of Hindu artistic traditions with local styles. Iconic features such as intricate carvings, ornate sculptures, and temple spires reflected the synthesis of Hindu motifs with the artistic expressions of regions traversed by the Silk Road.

Influence on Healing Practices and Ayurveda:

Hinduism's contributions extended to the realm of healing practices and medicinal knowledge. Ayurveda, the traditional system of medicine rooted in Hindu philosophy, made its way along the Silk Road. The exchange of herbal remedies, medicinal plants, and healing techniques enriched local medical practices. Ayurvedic principles, emphasizing holistic well-being, resonated with Silk Road communities and influenced the development of traditional medicine in those regions.

Astronomical Contributions:

The advanced astronomical knowledge present in Hindu texts found its way into the intellectual exchanges facilitated by the Silk Road. Scholars and astronomers from India shared insights into celestial observations, planetary movements, and mathematical calculations. This exchange contributed to the refinement of astronomical knowledge along the Silk

Road, impacting not only scientific thought but also navigational practices crucial for trade routes.

Cultural Festivals and Ritual Practices:

The celebration of Hindu festivals and ritual practices became integral to the cultural mosaic of Silk Road societies. Festivals like Diwali and Holi, characterized by vibrant celebrations, were adopted and adapted by communities along the trade routes. The colorful festivities and ritual practices fostered a sense of cultural camaraderie, contributing to a shared calendar of events that transcended religious affiliations.

Manuscript Transmission and Literary Contributions:

Hindu manuscripts, encompassing religious texts, literature, and scientific treatises, were transmitted along the Silk Road. The exchange of literary works facilitated not only the dissemination of religious ideas but also the sharing of philosophical treatises and epics. The Mahabharata and Ramayana, epic narratives central to Hinduism, found resonance and adaptations in the literary traditions of Silk Road cultures.

Cultural Diplomacy and Diplomatic Exchanges:

Hindu kingdoms and empires engaged in diplomatic relations with neighboring regions along the Silk Road. The exchange of envoys, gifts, and cultural emissaries fostered diplomatic ties and contributed to a sense of interconnectedness. Cultural diplomacy, exemplified by the exchange of art, artifacts, and intellectual pursuits, played a crucial role in shaping the diplomatic landscape along the Silk Road.

Hinduism's influence on the Silk Road was a dynamic process that unfolded across centuries, leaving an enduring legacy in the realms of spirituality, art, science, and cultural exchange. As a bridge between East and West, Hinduism not only contributed to the economic vitality of the Silk Road but also enriched the cultural and intellectual currents that flowed along this historic trade network.

Chapter 3: Maritime Marvels

In the expansive narrative of Hinduism, the maritime dimension emerges as a captivating chapter, revealing the profound impact of seafaring ventures on the dissemination of Hindu culture beyond the familiar shores of the Indian subcontinent. This exploration of ancient maritime trade becomes a testament to the enterprising spirit that propelled Hinduism's influence across distant oceans and seas.

This chapter delves into the seafaring endeavors that played a pivotal role in extending the reach of Hindu philosophy, traditions, and cultural richness to faraway lands. From bustling ports to vibrant maritime hubs, the narrative unveils the cultural exchanges, trade networks, and the enduring legacy of Hindu thought that unfolded along maritime routes. The seafaring heritage, etched in the annals of Hindu history, becomes a lens through which we unravel the intricate connections that bound civilizations, fostering a dynamic interplay of ideas and beliefs across the vast expanse of oceans and beyond.

Coastal Crossroads: Hinduism's Maritime Impact

The maritime dimension stands as a compelling narrative, embodying the far-reaching impact of seafaring ventures on the dissemination of Hindu culture and philosophy. This maritime odyssey, rooted in ancient times, not only facilitated trade but also served as a conduit for the diffusion of Hindu ideas, practices, and cultural nuances across the vast expanses of the Indian Ocean and beyond.

Maritime Trade Routes:

Hinduism's maritime impact is intricately woven into the fabric of historical trade routes. Ports along the western and eastern coasts of the Indian subcontinent, such as Bharuch, Kalyan, and Tamralipta, emerged as vibrant hubs connecting India to Southeast Asia, China, the Arabian Peninsula, and beyond. These maritime arteries facilitated the exchange of goods, ideas, and cultural practices, creating a dynamic network that linked diverse civilizations.

Cultural Exchanges:

The maritime endeavors of Hindu traders

and seafarers became conduits for profound cultural exchanges. As ships set sail, they carried not only spices, textiles, and precious commodities but also the intangible wealth of Hindu philosophy, art, and religious practices. This cultural diffusion left an enduring imprint on the societies and belief systems of regions touched by Hindu maritime activities.

Spread of Hindu Thought:

The maritime impact of Hinduism extended beyond economic and cultural exchanges to the dissemination of religious ideas. Temples dedicated to Hindu deities, built in distant lands, became symbols of spiritual continuity. Hindu cosmology, mythology, and ritual practices found resonance in regions as varied as Southeast Asia and the islands of the Indian Ocean, fostering a sense of shared religious heritage.

Architectural Marvels:

The architectural landscape along maritime trade routes bore witness to Hinduism's influence. Temples and structures built in regions influenced by Hindu maritime activities showcased a fusion of local architectural styles with distinct Hindu motifs. This syncretic blend created unique and awe-inspiring structures that endure as testaments to the cultural intermingling facilitated by seafaring connections.

Navigational Prowess:

Hindu seafarers, adept in maritime navigation, played a crucial role in connecting distant shores. Their navigational prowess, guided by ancient Hindu texts on astronomy and mathematics, enabled the successful navigation of vast oceans. This knowledge not only contributed to the safety and efficiency of trade routes but also fostered a deep connection between the maritime and intellectual pursuits of Hindu civilization.

Legacy of Cosmopolitanism:

The maritime impact of Hinduism fostered a cosmopolitan ethos, creating a shared cultural space that transcended geographical boundaries. It laid the foundation for a dynamic intercultural dialogue, enriching the civilizations that engaged in trade and cultural exchange with the Indian subcontinent.

In unraveling the narrative of Hinduism's maritime impact, we discover a legacy of connectivity, cultural diffusion, and intellectual exchange that shaped the contours of diverse societies along the maritime trade routes. The seas, once navigated by Hindu seafarers, became conduits of shared heritage, reflecting the enduring influence of Hinduism on the maritime tapestry of the ancient world.

Chola Naval Dominance: The Sea as a Channel for Cultural Exchange

In the annals of maritime history, the Chola dynasty emerges as a formidable force that not only wielded dominance over the seas but also harnessed the vast expanse of the Indian Ocean as a channel for profound cultural exchange. This epoch, spanning from the 9th to the 13th centuries, witnessed the Cholas' naval prowess extending across the Indian subcontinent to Southeast Asia, marking a golden era of maritime influence that transcended mere military conquests.

Naval Prowess and Maritime Empire:

The Chola dynasty, seated in the fertile lands of Tamil Nadu, leveraged its strategic coastal location to build an unparalleled naval fleet. The might of the Chola navy became a force to be reckoned with, extending its dominion over the Indian Ocean. This naval supremacy laid the foundation for an expansive maritime empire that reached distant shores, fostering both diplomatic ties and economic prosperity.

Trade and Economic Hub:

Chola naval dominance transformed the Indian Ocean into a thriving trade and economic hub. Ports such as Nagapattinam and Kaveripattinam became bustling centers, facilitating the exchange of goods, spices, textiles, and precious commodities with regions as far-reaching as the

Indonesian archipelago. The maritime Silk Road, under Chola influence, witnessed a flourishing trade network that contributed to the economic prosperity of both the Chola kingdom and its trading partners.

Cultural Synthesis Across Oceans:

Beyond military conquests and economic gains, the Chola navy acted as a bridge for extensive cultural exchanges. Hinduism, embedded in the Chola ethos, diffused across the sea routes, leaving an indelible imprint on the cultures of Southeast Asia. Temples built by the Cholas in regions like Cambodia and Indonesia stand as architectural marvels, reflecting the syncretic blend of Chola and indigenous cultural elements.

Architectural Marvels:

The Cholas, patrons of art and architecture, left an enduring legacy in the form of magnificent maritime-inspired structures. The Brihadeeswarar Temple in Thanjavur, a UNESCO World Heritage site, stands as a testament to Chola architectural prowess. Beyond the Indian shores, the Cholas built temples and monuments in territories influenced by their naval dominance, contributing to the cultural tapestry of regions such as Sri Lanka and Malaysia.

Cultural Diplomacy and Soft Power:

Chola naval dominance was not merely about military conquest; it was also a manifestation of cultural diplomacy. The Cholas exercised soft power, fostering diplomatic ties through cultural and religious exchanges. This cultural diplomacy created a lasting impact, engendering a sense of shared heritage and mutual respect among the diverse civilizations connected by the Chola maritime network.

Legacy of the Chola Maritime Era:

The Chola maritime era, characterized by naval dominance and cultural exchange, left an indelible mark on the history of the Indian Ocean. The legacy of this era endures in the maritime traditions, cultural syntheses, and architectural marvels that stand as a testament to the Cholas' profound impact on the seas as channels for cultural exchange.

In the wake of the Chola naval dominance, the Indian Ocean became not just a realm of conquest but a dynamic conduit for the diffusion of ideas, beliefs, and artistic expressions. The Cholas, through their mastery of the seas, forged a maritime legacy that transcended territorial boundaries, weaving together a rich tapestry of cultures across the vast expanse of the Indian Ocean.

Beyond the Monsoons: Maritime Trade Routes and Cultural Syncretism

a symphony of cultural syncretism unfolds, weaving together the diverse threads of civilizations that have navigated the waters of the world's oceans. The bustling arteries of sea trade have not merely facilitated the exchange of goods; they have also become conduits for a rich interplay of cultures, beliefs, and traditions. This tapestry of maritime trade routes resonates with the echoes of cultural syncretism, a harmonious blending of diverse influences that transcends geographical boundaries.

The Maritime Silk Road:

One of the most illustrious examples of maritime trade routes fostering cultural syncretism is the Maritime Silk Road. Spanning from the Mediterranean to the South China Sea, this network of sea routes facilitated the exchange of silk, spices, precious metals, and ideas. As merchants plied the waters, they carried not only tangible commodities but also the intangible wealth of cultural practices, philosophies, and artistic expressions.

Example: The ancient Maritime Silk Road connected the ports of Quanzhou in China to the bustling trade centers of Calicut in India and Aden in the Arabian Peninsula. This facilitated the exchange of Chinese silk, Indian spices, and Arabian incense, alongside the intermingling of cultural and religious ideas.

Spice Routes and Culinary Exchange:

The Spice Routes, connecting the Indian subcontinent to the Middle East and beyond, were not just conduits for aromatic treasures; they became channels for culinary exchange. Spices like pepper, cinnamon, and cardamom traveled along with recipes, culinary techniques, and dietary preferences. This exchange of flavors and cooking traditions left an indelible mark on the gastronomic landscapes of regions connected by maritime spice trade.

Example: The maritime Spice Routes enabled the transmission of spices such as cinnamon, pepper, and cardamom from the Indian subcontinent to the Middle East and Europe. This exchange influenced culinary practices, with Indian spices becoming integral to dishes in regions like Southeast

Asia and the Mediterranean.

Cultural Caravans of Ideas:

Maritime trade routes acted as cultural caravans, transporting ideas and intellectual pursuits across distant shores. Philosophies, religious beliefs, and scientific knowledge traversed the seas, fostering a cross-fertilization of thought. The exchange of manuscripts, artworks, and scholars contributed to the flourishing of centers of learning and cultural enlightenment in port cities along these routes.

Example: The translation of Indian mathematical texts into Arabic during the Abbasid Caliphate was facilitated by maritime trade connections. This intellectual exchange laid the groundwork for the transmission of mathematical knowledge to medieval Europe, contributing to the Renaissance.

Architectural Fusion in Port Cities:

Port cities, thriving at the crossroads of maritime trade, became melting pots of architectural styles. The cultural syncretism is evident in the unique blend of local traditions with influences from distant lands. Temples, mosques, and churches in port cities bear witness to the fusion of artistic motifs, architectural techniques, and religious symbolism brought together by the convergence of maritime cultures.

Example: The city of Melaka in Malaysia, a prominent port in the Maritime Silk Road, boasts architectural marvels reflecting a fusion of Chinese, Indian, and Islamic styles. The Cheng Hoon Teng Temple and

Kampung Kling Mosque exemplify this syncretic architectural blend.

Religious Tolerance and Coexistence:

Maritime trade routes nurtured an environment of religious tolerance and coexistence. Ports with diverse populations witnessed the establishment of religious spaces catering to various faiths. This inclusivity, born out of the necessity for harmonious trade relations, fostered a spirit of mutual respect and acceptance among communities with differing religious backgrounds.

Example: The port city of Kochi in India has been a melting pot of religious diversity due to maritime trade. It houses the Paradesi Synagogue, the oldest active synagogue in the Commonwealth of Nations, alongside ancient Hindu temples and Christian churches.

Artistic Fusion and Cultural Aesthetics:

Artistic expressions, influenced by the intermingling of cultures along maritime routes, resulted in a fusion of aesthetics. Sculptures, paintings, and decorative arts in port cities reflect a synthesis of artistic styles, motifs, and iconography. This blending of cultural aesthetics created a visual language that transcended regional boundaries.

Example: The Borobudur Temple in Indonesia, influenced by Indian Gupta and post-Gupta art, stands as a testament to the cultural fusion along maritime routes. The temple's reliefs depict scenes from Buddhist and Hindu cosmology, showcasing a blend of artistic traditions.

Linguistic Crossroads:

The linguistic landscape along maritime trade routes is marked by the crossroads of languages. Lingua franca, pidgin languages, and creole dialects emerged as means of communication among diverse communities engaged in trade. This linguistic exchange contributed to the richness and diversity of language along maritime routes.

Example: The development of Malay as a lingua franca in the Southeast Asian archipelago is a result of linguistic exchange along maritime routes. Malay, enriched by Sanskrit, Arabic, and Chinese influences, became a bridge for communication among diverse communities.

Musical Harmonies Across Oceans:

The movement of people and cultures along maritime trade routes gave rise to a harmonious exchange of musical traditions. Instruments, melodies, and rhythmic patterns traveled across the seas, influencing the evolution of musical styles in distant lands. The blending of diverse musical elements became a testament to the shared creativity that emerged from cultural encounters.

Example: The Gamelan music tradition in Indonesia, characterized by percussion instruments, has influences from Indian and Chinese musical styles. This cultural fusion in music is a testament to the cross-cultural harmonies shaped by maritime connections.

Fashion and Textile Cross-Cultural Influences:

The textile trade along maritime routes played a pivotal role in shaping fashion and clothing styles. Fabrics, weaving techniques, and garment designs traversed oceans, leading to a cross-cultural fusion of sartorial aesthetics. The vibrant tapestry of clothing traditions in port cities reflects the confluence of diverse textile traditions.

Example: The introduction of Indian chintz to Europe via maritime trade routes influenced European textile design in the 17th century. The vibrant floral patterns and intricate designs became highly sought after in European fashion.

Maritime Festivals and Celebrations:

Port cities, at the heart of maritime trade,

became stages for vibrant festivals and celebrations that mirrored the cultural diversity of the seafaring communities. These events, marked by music, dance, and rituals, showcased the synthesis of festive traditions from different regions, creating a unique and dynamic cultural calendar along the maritime routes.

Example: The Loy Krathong festival in Thailand, celebrated by floating decorated baskets on water, has elements derived from Hindu traditions brought by maritime trade. The festival showcases a cultural synthesis rooted in the maritime exchange.

Environmental Exchange and Ecological Impact:

Maritime trade routes not only facilitated the movement of goods and cultures but also led to an ecological exchange. The introduction of new flora and fauna, spurred by trade and exploration, transformed ecosystems in regions where different cultures converged. This environmental interchange further contributed to the complexity of cultural syncretism.

Example: The introduction of New World crops, such as maize and potatoes, to the Old World through maritime trade routes transformed agricultural practices and diets on a global scale, exemplifying the ecological impact of cultural syncretism.

Maritime Folklore and Nautical Narratives:

Seafaring communities, bound by maritime trade, shared not only commodities but also stories and folklore. Nautical narratives, myths, and legends traversed the waves alongside the merchant ships. These tales, passed down through generations, became a shared cultural heritage that transcended geographical origins.

Example: The Sinbad tales from Arabian Nights, influenced by Indian, Persian, and Greek stories, depict maritime adventures and showcase the cultural exchange of nautical narratives along trade routes.

Technological Innovation and Knowledge Transfer:

The maritime trade routes served as conduits for the transfer of technological innovations and knowledge. Navigational instruments, shipbuilding techniques, and scientific discoveries were disseminated across cultures. This exchange of practical knowledge contributed to advancements in various fields and enhanced the maritime capabilities of diverse seafaring communities.

Example: The compass, initially developed in China, spread to the Islamic world and Europe through maritime trade. This navigational instrument revolutionized seafaring and contributed to the interconnectedness of global cultures.

Diasporic Communities and Cultural Diaspora:

Maritime trade routes gave rise to diasporic communities that carried their cultural heritage to new lands. These communities, while maintaining connections with their ancestral cultures, also contributed to the cultural diversity of their adopted homes.

The amalgamation of traditions within diasporic communities exemplifies the enduring impact of maritime trade on cultural landscapes.

Example: The Indian diaspora in Southeast Asia, established through centuries of maritime trade, has preserved its cultural heritage while contributing to the diversity of cultures in countries like Malaysia, Singapore, and Indonesia.

In contemplating the vast and intricate web of maritime trade routes, one finds not only the exchange of tangible goods but also the profound intermingling of cultures, ideas, and expressions. The seas, as conduits for cultural syncretism, have shaped the shared human experience, fostering a global interconnectedness that transcends borders and resonates through the rich tapestry of our collective heritage.

Chapter 4: Temples in the Far East

In the unfolding narrative of cultural exchange along maritime trade routes, the Far East emerges as a canvas adorned with the architectural splendor and spiritual resonance of Hindu temples. This chapter delves into the intriguing legacy of temples in the Far East, where the maritime Silk Road became a conduit for the diffusion of Hindu religious and artistic traditions beyond the Indian subcontinent.

As maritime trade routes connected the bustling ports of the Indian subcontinent to the distant shores of Southeast Asia, China, and beyond, temples took root in foreign lands, becoming beacons of cultural syncretism. These temples, with their intricate carvings, towering spires, and sacred precincts, not only served as places of worship but also stood as living testimonials to the enduring influence of Hinduism on the spiritual landscapes of the Far East.

The journey of temples in the Far East unfolds against the backdrop of seafaring adventures, bustling trade, and the intermingling of diverse cultures. From the iconic Angkor Wat in Cambodia, with its Hindu origins evident in the dedication to Lord Vishnu, to the Prambanan Temple in Indonesia, adorned with intricate reliefs depicting episodes from Hindu epics, these architectural marvels mirror the cultural tapestry woven by maritime connections.

The Far East, enriched by the architectural

aesthetics and spiritual ethos of Hindu temples, bears witness to the syncretic blend of indigenous traditions with the cultural influx carried by the maritime Silk Road. Temples in this region not only signify places of devotion but also stand as cultural landmarks, embodying the enduring legacy of cultural and religious interchange that unfolded along the maritime trade routes. This exploration illuminates the role of temples as enduring symbols of cultural syncretism, inviting us to traverse the spiritual landscapes shaped by the tides of maritime exchange in the Far East.

Angkor Wat: The Jewel of Cambodian Hinduism

In the heart of Cambodia, the magnificent Angkor Wat stands as a testament to the grandeur of Cambodian Hinduism, a jewel that reflects the enduring cultural and religious legacy fostered by maritime trade routes. This colossal temple complex, nestled within the expansive Angkor Archaeological Park, encapsulates the richness of Hindu architectural and spiritual traditions against the backdrop of the lush Cambodian landscape.

Built in the early 12th century during the reign of King Suryavarman II, Angkor Wat was dedicated to the Hindu god Vishnu. The temple's architectural design, with its towering spires, intricate bas-reliefs, and expansive courtyards, embodies the essence of classical Khmer architecture deeply rooted in Hindu cosmology and mythology. The central towers represent Mount Meru, the abode of the gods in Hindu mythology, while the intricate carvings depict scenes from the Ramayana and Mahabharata.

The construction of Angkor Wat unfolded during a period when Cambodia was an integral part of the maritime Silk Road. Maritime trade routes facilitated not only the movement of goods but also the exchange of cultural and religious ideas. As a result, Angkor Wat emerged not only as a place of worship but also as a cultural nexus where influences from India, the Malay Archipelago, and beyond converged.

Despite the later shift of Cambodia's predominant religion to Theravada Buddhism, Angkor Wat remains a symbol of the profound impact of Hinduism on Cambodian culture. The temple's bas-reliefs, depicting Hindu deities and mythological narratives, are vivid testaments to the enduring legacy of Hindu iconography.

In the present day, Angkor Wat continues to draw visitors from across the globe, captivating them with its architectural splendor and spiritual ambiance. The temple's designation as a UNESCO World Heritage Site underscores its significance not only for Cambodia but for humanity as a whole. As we explore Angkor Wat, we unravel the layers of history woven into its stones, revealing a jewel that gleams with the cultural and spiritual exchanges fostered by the maritime connections of the ancient world.

Majestic Prambanan: Indonesia's Hindu Heritage

Nestled amidst the lush landscapes of Central Java, Indonesia, the majestic Prambanan temple complex emerges as a resplendent testament to the enduring legacy of Hinduism in the archipelago. Constructed in the 9th century during the Mataram Kingdom's reign, Prambanan stands as an architectural masterpiece and a cultural jewel that reflects Indonesia's deep connection to Hindu traditions fostered by maritime trade routes.

Architectural Splendor:

Prambanan's awe-inspiring complex comprises a cluster of towering temples, the most prominent being dedicated to the Trimurti – the Hindu trinity of Brahma, Vishnu, and Shiva. The main Shiva temple, with its soaring central spire reaching 47 meters, stands as a symbol of cosmic order and divine transcendence. Surrounding it are smaller temples dedicated to Vishnu, adorned with intricate carvings depicting scenes from the Ramayana and Mahabharata, and Brahma, the creator in

Hindu cosmology.

Cultural Syncretism and Maritime Connections:

Prambanan's construction unfolded during a period when Indonesia was a vital hub along the maritime Silk Road. Traders from India, China, and beyond sailed through the archipelago, bringing not only goods but also the cultural and religious tenets of Hinduism. Prambanan, with its fusion of indigenous Indonesian artistry and Hindu iconography, stands as a testament to the harmonious syncretism that blossomed along these maritime routes.

The Ramayana Narrative:

The temple's reliefs intricately narrate episodes from the Ramayana, showcasing the cultural convergence of Indian and

Indonesian storytelling traditions. The narrative unfolds in captivating detail, from the abduction of Sita to the epic battle between Rama and Ravana. Each carving is a masterpiece, conveying not just the religious significance but also the artistic prowess of the cultures that converged at Prambanan.

Decline and Restoration:

Over the centuries, Prambanan faced the challenges of time, natural disasters, and shifts in political power. The temple complex fell into disrepair and obscurity. However, in the 20th century, extensive restoration efforts spearheaded by Indonesian and international teams sought to revive Prambanan's former glory. The meticulous reconstruction aimed to recapture the intricate details and architectural magnificence of this Hindu heritage site.

Cultural Significance Today:

Designated as a UNESCO World Heritage Site, Prambanan stands as a living testament to Indonesia's rich cultural tapestry and its enduring ties to Hindu traditions. Pilgrims, tourists, and scholars alike flock to witness the grandeur of Prambanan, not only as a religious site but as a beacon of cultural exchange and syncretism that continues to resonate in the vibrant mosaic of Indonesia's diverse heritage.

Prambanan's Eternal Spirit:

As the sun sets behind the towering spires of Prambanan, casting a golden hue upon the ancient stones, the temple complex exudes an eternal spirit. It whispers tales of maritime journeys, cultural encounters, and the resilience of Indonesia's Hindu heritage. Prambanan's majesty invites us to traverse the corridors of time, where the echoes of the maritime Silk Road continue to resonate, and the soul of Indonesia's Hindu legacy finds eternal expression in stone and story.

Khmer Kingdoms and Beyond: Hindu Temples Across Southeast Asia

The ancient Khmer Kingdoms of Southeast Asia flourished as vibrant hubs of cultural and religious exchange, leaving an indelible mark on the region's landscape through the construction of awe-inspiring Hindu temples. From Cambodia's Angkor Wat to Thailand's Phanom Rung, the Khmer civilization's architectural prowess and religious fervor shaped a transcendent tapestry of temples that stood as testaments to the interconnectedness fostered by maritime trade routes.

Angkor Wat - Jewel of Cambodia:

At the heart of the Khmer Kingdom's legacy lies Angkor Wat, an architectural marvel and the largest religious monument in the world. Built in the 12th century under the rule of King Suryavarman II, Angkor Wat's intricate design mirrors Mount Meru, the cosmic abode of the gods in Hindu mythology. Its vast complex, adorned with mesmerizing bas-reliefs and towering spires, became a center for worship and cultural convergence along the maritime Silk Road.

Bayon - Faces of Divinity in Cambodia:

Adjacent to Angkor Wat stands the Bayon

temple, a unique testament to Khmer artistry. This temple, constructed by King Jayavarman VII, is renowned for its iconic stone faces, believed to represent Bodhisattva Avalokiteshvara or a combination of Buddha and the king himself. Bayon's fusion of Hindu and Buddhist elements exemplifies the religious syncretism that characterized the Khmer Kingdom's cultural landscape.

Phanom Rung - Resplendent Sanctuary in Thailand:

Venturing beyond Cambodia, the influence of Khmer culture extended into Thailand, evident in the magnificent temple complex of Phanom Rung. Built between the 10th and 13th centuries, this sanctuary atop an extinct volcano reflects the Khmer devotion to Shiva. Its alignment with solar events demonstrates the Khmer's advanced understanding of astronomy, showcasing the integration of science and spirituality.

Prambanan - Java's Sacred Splendor:

Moving further southeast to Java, Indonesia, the Prambanan temple complex unfolds as a masterpiece of Hindu architecture. Built in the 9th century, Prambanan boasts towering spires dedicated to the Trimurti - Shiva, Vishnu, and Brahma. The temples, adorned with intricate carvings, narrate episodes from the Ramayana, attesting to the enduring legacy of Hindu epics across maritime routes.

My Son - Echoes of Champa Kingdom in Vietnam:

In Vietnam, the Champa Kingdom embraced Khmer architectural influence, evident in the My Son temple complex. Constructed between the 4th and 14th centuries, these temples dedicated to Shiva highlight the cultural diffusion and religious symbiosis that characterized Southeast Asian civilizations engaged in maritime trade.

Legacy of Maritime Syncretism:

The Khmer Kingdoms' expansion and cultural efflorescence were intrinsically linked to maritime trade routes. The exchange of goods and ideas facilitated by seafaring connections nurtured the flowering of Hindu culture across Southeast Asia. The temples, with their intricate carvings, celestial alignments, and religious motifs, became embodiments of a shared spiritual heritage that transcended political boundaries.

Cultural Resilience and Preservation:

While the decline of the Khmer Kingdoms and the shift to Theravada Buddhism marked a transformation in religious landscapes, the Hindu temples endured as cultural landmarks. Today, these temples stand not only as religious sites but also as living chronicles of the maritime Silk Road's profound impact on Southeast Asian civilizations.

In unraveling the intricate story of Khmer Kingdoms and beyond, we encounter a tapestry woven by the threads of maritime trade, cultural syncretism, and spiritual devotion. The temples, scattered across the region, invite us to traverse the realms of history and appreciate the enduring legacy of the Khmer civilization, whose architectural and cultural contributions resonate across the landscapes of

Southeast Asia.

Chapter 5: The Himalayan Haven

Nestled amidst the towering peaks and cradled in the embrace of the world's mightiest mountains, the Himalayas stand as a majestic haven, a realm where nature's grandeur converges with cultural richness. This towering mountain range, often referred to as the "Abode of Snow," extends its colossal arms across multiple countries, weaving a tapestry of landscapes, traditions, and spiritual sanctuaries. In this Himalayan haven, every valley, every soaring peak, and every winding river is a testament to both the awe-inspiring power of nature and the enduring resilience of human civilization.

As we embark on a journey through the Himalayas, we find ourselves immersed in a sanctuary of diverse cultures, where ancient traditions have thrived in the shadow of towering summits. From the prayer-flag adorned monasteries of Tibet to the terraced fields of Nepal, and the sacred rivers of India, the Himalayan region unfolds as a crucible of cultural exchange shaped by centuries of pilgrimage, trade, and spiritual exploration.

But the Himalayas are more than a mere canvas for human endeavors; they are a sanctuary for serenity and introspection. Amidst the whispering winds and the snow-capped peaks, Himalayan hermitages and retreats have been sanctuaries for seekers and sages. The tranquil monasteries perched on high ridges echo with the chants of monks, while the pristine lakes cradle reflections of towering peaks in their crystal-clear waters, inviting contemplation and spiritual renewal.

In this introduction to the Himalayan Haven, we embark on a literary ascent, tracing the contours of this sacred expanse. From the icy reaches of the Tibetan Plateau to the lush valleys of Bhutan, and the alpine meadows of Kashmir, we traverse a terrain that has not only shaped the physical geography of Asia but has also carved deep into the spiritual and cultural fabric of the communities dwelling in its shadow.

As we navigate this Himalayan haven, we shall explore the symbiotic relationship between nature and culture, delve into the rich tapestry of myths and legends that echo through the mountain passes, and pay homage to the communities that have carved out a life in the challenging yet enchanting embrace of the Himalayas.

Sacred Peaks: Hinduism in the Himalayan Foothills

In the foothills of the Himalayas, where the air is infused with the scent of rhododendron blooms and the symphony of mountain streams, Hinduism unfolds as an integral thread in the vibrant tapestry of cultures that call these sacred slopes home. This region, characterized by lush valleys, terraced fields, and sacred rivers, bears witness to a profound interweaving of Hindu traditions with the mystical allure of the Himalayan landscape.

Sacred Confluences:

The foothills of the Himalayas, known as the

Devabhumi or "Land of the Gods," cradle numerous pilgrimage sites and sacred confluences. Rivers like the Ganges, Yamuna, and Saraswati, flowing from the icy heights, meander through these foothills, sanctifying the land and nurturing the spiritual consciousness of the communities dwelling along their banks. Haridwar and Rishikesh, where the Ganges descends from the mountains to the plains, stand as epicenters of Hindu pilgrimage and spiritual fervor.

Rishikesh - The Yogic Gateway:

Rishikesh, nestled on the banks of the Ganges, emerges as a pulsating center of Hindu spirituality. Known as the "Yoga Capital of the World," this tranquil town has attracted seekers and sages for centuries. Ashrams and temples dot its riverbanks, offering havens for introspection and yogic practice. The iconic suspension bridge, Laxman Jhula, echoes with the footsteps of pilgrims and the chants of devotees as they traverse the sacred river.

Gangotri and Yamunotri - Source of Divine Waters:

High in the Himalayan reaches, the sacred shrines of Gangotri and Yamunotri mark the origins of the Ganges and Yamuna rivers. Pilgrims embark on arduous journeys to these lofty heights, seeking the blessings of these pristine waters that are believed to cleanse the soul. The Yamunotri temple, dedicated to the goddess Yamuna, and the Gangotri temple, venerating the Ganges, stand as testimony to the reverence bestowed upon these life-giving rivers.

Kedarnath and Badrinath - Abodes of Divine Presence:

As one ascends further into the Himalayas, the revered shrines of Kedarnath and Badrinath come into view. Kedarnath, dedicated to Lord Shiva, and Badrinath, dedicated to Lord Vishnu, are part of the Char Dham pilgrimage circuit. Surrounded by snow-capped peaks, these temples evoke a sense of divine transcendence and have been beacons for spiritual seekers navigating the lofty heights.

Nanda Devi and Hemkund Sahib - Mystical Heights:

The mystical heights of the Himalayas embrace sacred peaks like Nanda Devi, revered as the patron goddess of the region. Nearby, the pristine Hemkund Sahib, a high-altitude Sikh pilgrimage site, sits beside a glacial lake surrounded by seven peaks, exemplifying the harmonious coexistence of diverse religious traditions in the Himalayan foothills.

Cultural Festivals and Melas:

The Himalayan foothills resonate with the vibrant hues of cultural festivals and melas. The Kumbh Mela, hosted at various locations including Haridwar and Allahabad, draws millions of pilgrims for a sacred dip in the holy rivers. These gatherings become forums for spiritual discourse, cultural celebrations, and the forging of connections that transcend the diverse linguistic and cultural tapestry of the region.

In the heart of the Himalayan foothills, Hinduism breathes in rhythm with the mountain breeze, carving sacred spaces that echo with centuries of devotion and spiritual exploration. As we traverse these foothills, we encounter not only temples and rivers but also a profound intertwining of nature and divinity. The rituals, the chants, and the sacred landscapes become chapters in the sacred narrative that unfolds in the lap of the mighty Himalayas, inviting all who venture here to partake in the sanctity of this mystical haven.

Pilgrimage Paths: Spiritual Journeys in the Himalayan Landscape

In the heart of the majestic Himalayas, where lofty peaks touch the heavens and serene valleys cradle ancient secrets, spiritual journeys unfold as profound odysseys of self-discovery and transcendence. The Himalayan landscape, with its snow-clad summits, meandering rivers, and sacred groves, becomes a sacred canvas upon which seekers from diverse traditions paint their spiritual narratives. Embarking on a journey through this awe-inspiring terrain, one encounters not only the grandeur of nature but also the rich tapestry of spiritual exploration that has thrived for millennia.

Pilgrimages Along Sacred Rivers:

The Himalayan rivers, revered as goddesses, carve spiritual pathways through the rugged terrain. Pilgrims embark on transformative journeys along the Ganges, Yamuna, and Saraswati, seeking purification and divine blessings. The Gomukh glacier, the source of the Ganges, becomes a starting point for pilgrims on their sacred yatra, culminating at the Gangotri temple. The spiritual echoes of these riverine pilgrimages resound through the valleys, becoming a hymn to the sacredness of flowing waters.

Haridwar and Rishikesh - Gateway to the Divine:

Haridwar, where the Ganges descends from the mountains, and Rishikesh, nestled on its banks, emerge as gateways to the divine in the Himalayan landscape. The ghats of Haridwar witness the mesmerizing Ganga Aarti, a celestial dance of fire and devotion that draws pilgrims from far and wide. Rishikesh, with its ashrams and yoga retreats, becomes a haven for seekers, inviting them to explore the depths of their spiritual selves against the backdrop of the sacred river.

Amarnath Yatra - A Himalayan Pilgrimage:

In the higher reaches of the Himalayas, the Amarnath cave becomes a destination for an annual pilgrimage. Devotees undertake a challenging trek to witness the naturally occurring ice Shiva Lingam, believed to manifest during the auspicious months. The arduous journey becomes a metaphor for the trials and tribulations encountered on the path to spiritual realization.

Char Dham Yatra - Pilgrimage of Four Abodes:

The Char Dham Yatra, comprising Yamunotri, Gangotri, Kedarnath, and Badrinath, stands as a sacred circuit in the Himalayas. Pilgrims traverse these sacred sites, seeking blessings from the deities enshrined in each temple. The journey, often embarked upon by foot, becomes an odyssey of devotion, endurance, and communion with the divine forces that shape the Himalayan landscape.

Dharamshala and McLeod Ganj - Tibetan Spiritual Refuge:

In the western Himalayas, Dharamshala and McLeod Ganj become refuge points for Tibetan spiritual leaders, including His Holiness the Dalai Lama. The Tibetan monasteries, such as Tsuglagkhang and Namgyal Monastery, resonate with the chants of Buddhist monks and offer seekers a glimpse into the rich tapestry of Tibetan Buddhism flourishing in the Himalayan folds.

Sages of the Himalayas - Cave Retreats and Ashrams:

The Himalayas have long been a haven for sages and ascetics seeking solitude and communion with the divine. Cave retreats, such as the sacred caves of Tapovan and Vashisht, become abodes for meditation and spiritual contemplation. Ashrams dot the mountainsides, where seekers immerse themselves in the teachings of enlightened masters, forging a connection with the eternal wisdom that echoes through the Himalayan heights.

Kailash Mansarovar - Sacred Axis Mundi:

Mount Kailash, revered by Hindus, Buddhists, Jains, and Bon practitioners, stands as an iconic symbol of spiritual significance. The circumambulation, or Kora, around the sacred mountain and the pilgrimage to Mansarovar Lake become rites of passage, marking spiritual rebirth and the attainment of higher consciousness.

In the Himalayan landscape, spiritual journeys transcend the physical realm, becoming soul-stirring odysseys that unravel the mysteries of existence. Whether along the riverbanks, amidst the snow-capped peaks, or in the solace of ancient caves, seekers find a sanctuary for the soul, where the boundaries between the material and the spiritual dissolve into the timeless embrace of the Himalayas.

Tibetan Buddhism and Hindu Syncretism: An Interplay of Traditions

In the lofty plateaus of Tibet, where prayer flags flutter in the thin mountain air and monasteries cling to rugged cliffs, a unique interplay of spiritual traditions unfolds. Tibetan Buddhism, with its rich tapestry of rituals, iconography, and philosophy, engages in a harmonious dance with the ancient Hindu traditions that have permeated the Himalayan region. This interplay of traditions, marked by syncretism and mutual influence, creates a spiritual landscape where the boundaries between Tibetan Buddhism and Hinduism blur, fostering a vibrant and nuanced spiritual ethos.

Historical Roots:

The confluence of Tibetan Buddhism and Hinduism can be traced back to historical interactions between the Tibetan plateau and the Indian subcontinent. During the spread of Buddhism in the first millennium CE, Tibetan scholars and monks traveled to India to study Buddhist scriptures and philosophy. This exchange led to the assimilation of Hindu elements into Tibetan Buddhist practices.

Padmasambhava and Guru Rinpoche:

Central to the synthesis of these traditions

is the revered figure of Padmasambhava, also known as Guru Rinpoche. This Indian sage and tantric master played a pivotal role in the establishment of Buddhism in Tibet in the 8th century. Guru Rinpoche's teachings seamlessly integrated tantric practices, which were rooted in Indian traditions, with Tibetan Buddhist doctrines. His transformative presence is still felt in the Padmasambhava-inspired monasteries and rituals across Tibet.

Deities and Iconography:

One of the striking elements of syncretism is the shared pantheon of deities and iconography between Tibetan Buddhism and Hinduism. Deities like Avalokiteshvara, Tara, and Manjushri, commonly venerated in Tibetan Buddhism, have counterparts in Hinduism—Guanyin, Green Tara, and Saraswati, respectively. This shared imagery reflects a cultural and spiritual cross-fertilization that has occurred over centuries.

Sacred Texts and Mantras:

Tibetan Buddhism and Hinduism also share common sacred texts and mantras. The recitation of mantras, such as the universally known "Om Mani Padme Hum" in Tibetan Buddhism and the "Om Namah Shivaya" in Hinduism, exemplifies the convergence of devotional practices. Both traditions emphasize the transformative power of sound in invoking spiritual energies.

Wheel of Life and Samsara:

Concepts of the Wheel of Life (Bhavachakra) and the cycle of Samsara are fundamental to both traditions. Tibetan

Buddhist thangkas often depict the Wheel of Life, illustrating the cyclical nature of existence, a concept that resonates with the Hindu understanding of reincarnation and the eternal cycle of birth and rebirth.

Monastic Practices and Festivals:

Monastic practices in Tibetan Buddhism, including rituals, chanting, and elaborate ceremonies, draw inspiration from the Hindu tradition. Festivals such as Losar, the Tibetan New Year, are celebrated with fervor, blending indigenous Tibetan customs with ancient Hindu festival practices, reflecting the diverse cultural heritage of the region.

Yogic Practices and Meditation:

Both Tibetan Buddhism and Hinduism place a significant emphasis on yogic practices and meditation. The meditative techniques, breathing exercises, and visualization methods employed in Tibetan Buddhism find parallels in the yogic traditions of Hinduism. The shared goal of transcending the mundane and attaining spiritual enlightenment unites these diverse paths.

Cultural Festivals and Celebrations:

In regions where Tibetan Buddhism and Hinduism coexist, cultural festivals and celebrations often amalgamate elements from both traditions. This syncretic fusion is evident in processions, rituals, and artistic expressions that seamlessly integrate the diverse cultural and spiritual influences of the Himalayan landscape.

Unity in Diversity:

The interplay of Tibetan Buddhism and

Hindu syncretism reflects a remarkable unity in diversity, where spiritual seekers navigate a landscape enriched by multiple traditions. Rather than existing as separate entities, these traditions coalesce, creating a spiritual mosaic that resonates with the ethos of unity and interconnectedness—the very essence of the Himalayan region.

In the high altitudes of Tibet, where prayer flags flutter against the backdrop of towering peaks, the interplay of Tibetan Buddhism and Hindu syncretism unfolds as a living testament to the fluidity of spiritual traditions. This harmonious dance, echoing through monasteries, mountain passes, and sacred ceremonies, invites seekers to embrace a rich and nuanced tapestry that transcends the boundaries of individual faiths, embodying the timeless spirit of spiritual exploration in the Himalayas.

Chapter 6: African Threads

In the intricate weave of global history and cultural exchange, threads of Hinduism extend far beyond the Indian subcontinent, reaching unexpected corners of the world. One such intriguing tapestry unfolds in the vast and diverse landscapes of Africa, where the threads of Hindu influence intertwine with the rich fabric of indigenous traditions. As we embark on a journey through this lesser-explored chapter of cultural diffusion, we unravel the connections that bind Hinduism to the African continent.

The narrative of African Threads invites us to explore the intersections of spirituality, trade, and migration, where Hindu communities established themselves in various African regions. From the shores of the Indian Ocean to the inland realms, we discover how Hindu practices, beliefs, and cultural nuances found resonance amid the diverse ethnicities and belief systems of Africa. Through temple architecture, rituals, and the echoes of ancient stories, we trace the enduring impact of Hinduism, leaving an indelible mark on the cultural mosaic that defines Africa. We trace the enduring threads that connect the sacred traditions of Hinduism with the rich and diverse cultures of Africa. Through tales of migration, cultural syncretism, and shared spiritual wisdom.

East African Enigma: Hinduism's Presence in Ancient Societies

In the sun-kissed landscapes of East Africa,

where the savannah meets the Indian Ocean, an enigmatic chapter unfolds—a narrative of Hinduism's presence in ancient societies that has left an indelible mark on the cultural canvas of the region. From the maritime exchanges along the Indian Ocean to the migration of diverse communities, the threads of Hindu traditions wove seamlessly into the fabric of East African societies, creating a tapestry of religious syncretism and cultural diversity.

Maritime Trade Routes:

Centuries before the European colonial era, East Africa was a crucial node along the maritime trade routes that connected the Indian subcontinent with the African coast. These trade connections facilitated not only the exchange of goods but also the transmission of cultural and religious influences. Hindu traders, sailors, and settlers left an imprint on the coastal regions, contributing to the fusion of local African traditions with the spiritual tapestry of Hinduism.

Swahili Coast and Coastal City-States:

The Swahili Coast, with its bustling city-states, emerged as a melting pot of diverse cultures. Cities like Kilwa, Sofala, and Zanzibar became vibrant hubs where African, Arab, and Indian influences converged. Hindu merchants played a pivotal role in these cosmopolitan centers, contributing to the cultural and religious syncretism that defined the Swahili Coast's rich history.

Kilwa Kisiwani: A Crossroads of Cultures:

Kilwa Kisiwani, an island off the Tanzanian coast, stands as a testament to the intermingling of cultures. Archaeological evidence reveals the presence of Hindu-style stone temples and pillars, suggesting a cultural exchange that transcended religious boundaries. The Great Mosque of Kilwa, an architectural marvel, showcases a fusion of local African and foreign influences, embodying the syncretic spirit of the region.

Migration and Settlement:

The migration of Indian and Arab communities to East Africa further deepened the roots of Hinduism in the region. These settlers brought with them not only their religious practices but also their cultural traditions, influencing the local ethos. The establishment of Hindu temples, like the one in Mombasa, became centers for spiritual sustenance and cultural preservation.

Cultural Syncretism:

East Africa became a crucible of cultural syncretism, where Hindu rituals, festivals, and artistic expressions melded with indigenous African customs. Elements of Hindu mythology found resonance in local stories, and deities from both traditions became intertwined in the spiritual consciousness of East African communities.

Legacy in Modern Times:

While the historical presence of Hinduism in East Africa is evident in archaeological findings and cultural artifacts, its legacy endures in modern times. Hindu festivals, practices, and cultural celebrations continue to be cherished by communities along the East African coast, reflecting a shared history that transcends temporal and spatial boundaries.

Challenges and Resilience:

The narrative of Hinduism in East Africa also encompasses challenges faced by these communities, including cultural assimilation and, at times, tensions with other religious traditions. Yet, the resilience of these communities in preserving their cultural and religious heritage underscores the enduring significance of Hinduism in the East African tapestry.

Hinduism's presence in ancient East African societies is not merely a historical artifact but a living testament to the resilience and adaptability of cultural traditions. The East African enigma invites us to explore the threads that bind diverse cultures, revealing a shared human heritage shaped by the interplay of ancient civilizations across the Indian Ocean.

Madagascar's Mystique: Tracing Hindu Traditions in Isolation

In the vast expanse of the Indian Ocean, ensconced in the embrace of azure waters, lies the enigmatic island of Madagascar. Far removed from the bustling trade routes and ancient crossroads, Madagascar's isolation has woven a unique tapestry of cultures, where the threads of Hindu traditions have quietly thrived in the island's mystique. This isolated haven, with its lush landscapes and diverse ecosystems, unveils a narrative of resilience and cultural preservation that transcends the sands of time.

A Journey Across the Indian Ocean:

Madagascar's story begins with the maritime journeys that traversed the Indian Ocean. The Malagasy people, believed to have originated from Southeast Asia, navigated the ocean currents, carrying with them not only their physical presence but also the intangible threads of cultural practices and spiritual beliefs. The island's isolation, surrounded by vast stretches of water, allowed these traditions to evolve in a unique and uninterrupted manner.

Cultural Syncretism:

As the Malagasy people settled on the island, they encountered a tapestry of indigenous beliefs and practices. In this cultural crossroads, Hindu traditions found a space for syncretism, blending with the island's animistic and indigenous belief systems. Elements of Hindu cosmology, deities, and rituals seamlessly interwove with local customs, giving rise to a distinctive Malagasy-Hindu synthesis.

Sacred Sites and Temples:

Madagascar's landscape is dotted with sacred sites and temples that bear witness to the enduring presence of Hindu traditions. The Ambalavao region, for instance, is home to the Ambohipotsy temple, a place of worship where rituals echoing Hindu practices are performed. These temples, nestled amidst the island's natural beauty, serve as both spiritual sanctuaries and cultural landmarks.

Ancestor Worship and Cosmic Beliefs:

The intricate Malagasy practice of ancestor worship, deeply ingrained in the island's cultural fabric, finds resonance with certain Hindu beliefs. The veneration of ancestors as spiritual intermediaries and the belief in a cosmic connection between the living and the departed echo Hindu cosmological concepts, creating a spiritual harmony that defies geographical isolation.

Cultural Artefacts and Oral Traditions:

Madagascar's mystique is also preserved in its cultural artifacts and oral traditions. Traditional dances, stories, and art forms reflect the subtle influence of Hindu aesthetics and narratives. The retelling of ancient epics and the use of symbolic motifs in art reveal the enduring impact of Hindu culture on the artistic expressions of the Malagasy people.

Challenges and Preservation:

Madagascar's Hindu traditions, existing in relative isolation, have faced challenges over the centuries. Colonial influences, external cultural pressures, and changing demographics have posed threats to the preservation of these traditions. Yet, the resilience of the Malagasy people in safeguarding their cultural heritage speaks to the enduring spirit of cultural preservation.

A Living Heritage:

As we unravel Madagascar's mystique, we encounter not merely remnants of a bygone era but a living heritage that continues to shape the identity of the Malagasy people. Hindu traditions, interwoven with the island's cultural fabric, stand as a testament to the power of cultural endurance and adaptation in the face of isolation.

Madagascar's mystique, with its lush landscapes and cultural amalgamation, invites us to contemplate the intricate interplay of Hindu traditions in the most unexpected corners of the world. In tracing these threads of cultural resilience and adaptation, we discover a narrative that transcends isolation, revealing the universal spirit of human ingenuity and the enduring allure of Madagascar's mystique.

Afro-Indian Encounters: The Intersection of Cultures in Ancient Africa

In the annals of ancient history, where the African continent meets the Indian subcontinent, a captivating narrative unfolds—a story of Afro-Indian encounters that have shaped the cultural landscapes of both regions. Beyond the geographical expanse that separates these lands, ancient Africa became a convergence point for diverse cultures, fostering exchanges that transcended borders and oceans. This exploration delves into the rich tapestry of interactions, trade, and cultural syncretism that marked the intersection of African and Indian civilizations.

Maritime Silk Routes:

The maritime silk routes, spanning from the Indian Ocean to the coastlines of East Africa, acted as conduits for cultural exchanges between these two ancient worlds. The Indian Ocean, often referred to as the "Monsoon Marketplace," witnessed the ebb and flow of traders, sailors, and settlers who traversed the seas, bringing with them not only goods but also a rich tapestry of beliefs, traditions, and artistic expressions.

Trade and Economic Exchanges:

At the heart of Afro-Indian encounters lay a vibrant trade network that connected the bustling ports of the Indian subcontinent with the flourishing city-states along the East African coast. Spices, textiles, gemstones, and ivory were exchanged for gold, exotic animals, and other commodities. This economic interdependence laid the foundation for deeper cultural interactions.

Swahili Coast and Cosmopolitan Centers:

The Swahili Coast, with its bustling city-states like Kilwa, Sofala, and Mombasa, emerged as cosmopolitan centers where African, Arab, and Indian influences intersected. These cities became crucibles of cultural syncretism, where Afro-Indian communities coexisted, intermingling their languages, cuisines, and religious practices.

Architectural Marvels:

The architectural marvels along the Swahili Coast bear testimony to the intersection of Afro-Indian cultures. Intricate designs of coral stone structures, characterized by Arab, Persian, and Indian influences, adorn the coastal cities. Mosques with minarets reminiscent of Indian architecture stand alongside Swahili-style houses, creating a visual testament to the fusion of diverse artistic traditions.

Religious Syncretism:

Afro-Indian encounters profoundly influenced the religious landscape of East Africa. Islam, introduced by Arab and Indian traders, found a fertile ground, blending with indigenous African belief systems. The Swahili Coast became a crucible where Sufi traditions, Hindu practices, and African spirituality coexisted, creating a syncretic spiritual ethos.

Cultural Diffusion:

Beyond the coastal regions, Afro-Indian encounters left an indelible mark on the interiors of East Africa. Cultural diffusion manifested in the adoption of Indian agricultural practices, cuisine, and clothing styles. The introduction of crops like rice and sugarcane, as well as the use of spices in local cuisines, reflected the enduring impact of these cultural exchanges.

Language and Literature:

Linguistic influences also permeated Afro-Indian encounters. Swahili, a language that evolved as a result of interactions between Bantu-speaking communities and Arab and Indian traders, stands as a linguistic synthesis. Literary traditions, including the Swahili epic poetry of "Utendi wa

Tambuka," showcase the melding of African and Indian narrative styles.

Challenges and Resilience:

While Afro-Indian encounters brought about cultural flourishing, they also faced challenges. External pressures, such as European colonization, disrupted these exchanges, posing threats to the preservation of the rich cultural tapestry that had evolved over centuries. Yet, the resilience of Afro-Indian communities in preserving their heritage amidst adversity speaks to the enduring spirit of cultural identity.

Legacy in Modern Africa:

The legacy of Afro-Indian encounters reverberates in the cultural diversity of modern Africa. From the Swahili Coast to the hinterlands, traces of Indian influences endure in language, cuisine, and religious practices. Afro-Indian communities continue to contribute to the cultural vibrancy of the region, embodying a living testament to the enduring connections forged in ancient times.

Afro-Indian encounters, situated at the crossroads of ancient civilizations, unfold as a fascinating chapter in the shared history of Africa and the Indian subcontinent. In exploring the intersection of cultures, this narrative invites us to contemplate the resilience, adaptability, and richness that emerged from these encounters—a legacy that transcends temporal and geographical boundaries, embodying the interconnectedness of human civilizations across the ages.

Chapter 7: Island Reverberations

Amidst the vast expanses of oceans, where azure waters cradle isolated islands, a mystical resonance echoes through time—a testament to the enduring presence of Hinduism in distant paradises. This exploration embarks on a captivating journey to uncover the threads of Hindu traditions that have woven themselves into the cultural fabric of these secluded realms. From the Indian subcontinent to remote shores, delve into the captivating stories of how Hinduism, like a sacred breeze, has touched the hearts and landscapes of far-flung islands.

Beyond the bustling mainland, these islands

stand as testaments to the cultural diaspora carried by ancient seafarers and traders. Through maritime routes and cultural exchanges, Hinduism's sacred rituals, mythologies, and architectural aesthetics have left an indelible mark on islands scattered across the Indian Ocean. Unravel the tales of sacred temples amidst palm-fringed shores, where the confluence of diverse cultures has given rise to unique syntheses, forging a connection between the mainland and these isolated realms.

Sri Lanka's Hindu Heritage: A Tapestry of Tamil Traditions

In the island nation of Sri Lanka, where verdant landscapes meet azure shores, a vibrant tapestry of Hindu heritage unfolds—a testament to the enduring legacy of Tamil traditions that have shaped the cultural mosaic of this enchanting land. Amidst the palm-fringed coastlines and lush hills, Sri Lanka's Hindu heritage stands as a testament to the resilience and vibrancy of the Tamil communities that have contributed to the island's rich cultural diversity.

Historical Roots:

Sri Lanka's Hindu heritage traces its roots back to ancient times, with connections to the flourishing Tamil civilizations of South India. The arrival of Tamil settlers and traders to the island established a cultural bridge that endured through centuries, fostering a unique synthesis of Dravidian traditions against the backdrop of Sri Lanka's natural beauty.

Temples and Sacred Sites:

The landscape of Sri Lanka is adorned with sacred temples dedicated to Hindu deities, each bearing witness to the deep spiritual roots embedded in the island's soil. The Nallur Kandaswamy Kovil in Jaffna, the Koneswaram Temple in Trincomalee, and the Munneswaram Kovil near Chilaw are among the revered sites that echo with prayers and rituals, serving as sanctuaries for the island's Hindu community.

Cultural Syncretism:

Sri Lanka's Hindu heritage is characterized by a harmonious blend of Tamil traditions with indigenous Sri Lankan customs. This cultural syncretism is evident in festivals such as Thaipusam and Maha Shivaratri, where vibrant processions, elaborate rituals, and devotional music become expressions of shared spirituality that transcends religious boundaries.

Language and Literature:

The Tamil language, with its rich literary traditions, has played a pivotal role in preserving and transmitting Sri Lanka's Hindu heritage. Ancient Tamil texts, including the Sangam literature, have found a cherished place in the cultural tapestry of the island, fostering a linguistic and literary continuity with South Indian Tamil traditions.

Art and Architecture:

The artistic expressions of Sri Lanka's Hindu heritage manifest in the intricate sculptures, vibrant murals, and majestic architecture of its temples. The intricate carvings at the Ketheeswaram Kovil and the imposing tower of the Nallur Kandaswamy Kovil are testaments to the skilled craftsmanship that has flourished in tandem with spiritual devotion.

Cultural Celebrations:

Festivals and celebrations form an integral part of Sri Lanka's Hindu heritage. The grand chariot festival at the Nallur Kovil, the colorful Vel Festival, and the exuberant Pongal celebrations reflect the island's dynamic cultural calendar. These events not only serve as religious observances but also foster a sense of community and shared identity.

Challenges and Resilience:

Sri Lanka's Hindu heritage has faced challenges over the centuries, including periods of political upheaval and conflict. Despite these challenges, the resilience of the Tamil Hindu community has been evident in their unwavering commitment to preserving their cultural practices, rituals, and spiritual traditions.

Legacy and Modern Times:

As Sri Lanka strides into the modern era, the legacy of its Hindu heritage endures as an integral part of the nation's cultural diversity. The Tamil Hindu communities continue to contribute to the island's social fabric, enriching the collective identity of Sri Lanka with their deep-rooted traditions.

Sri Lanka's Hindu heritage, intricately woven into the cultural fabric of the island, stands as a testament to the enduring spirit of Tamil traditions. This tapestry of heritage, shaped by centuries of historical interactions, cultural syncretism, and spiritual devotion, invites us to explore the rich and diverse expressions of Hinduism that have thrived against the backdrop of Sri Lanka's tropical landscapes.

Malayan Archipelago: Hindu Influences in Malaysia and Beyond

In the heart of the Malayan Archipelago, where emerald waters embrace a myriad of islands, a cultural tapestry unfolds, woven with the threads of Hindu influences that have left an indelible mark on the landscapes of Malaysia and beyond. This exploration delves into the historical corridors of time, tracing the ebb and flow of cultural exchanges that have enriched the region, creating a vibrant mosaic where Hindu traditions have seamlessly blended with the diverse cultures of Southeast Asia.

Early Maritime Connections:

The maritime routes connecting the Indian subcontinent with the Malayan Archipelago served as conduits for cultural exchanges. Traders, seafarers, and settlers navigated these waters, bringing with them not only goods but also the intangible wealth of Hindu religious and cultural practices. The early Hindu-Buddhist kingdoms of Srivijaya and Majapahit in present-day Indonesia stand as testament to the flourishing civilization that emerged from these exchanges.

Ancient Kingdoms and Empires:

The Indianization of the region, facilitated by trade and diplomatic ties, gave rise to powerful Hindu-Buddhist empires. In Malaysia, the historical kingdom of Langkasuka, followed by the powerful Srivijaya Empire, established a cultural milieu influenced by Indian epics, art, and governance systems. The architectural marvels of Borobudur in Java and Prambanan in Indonesia reflect the grandeur of Hindu-Buddhist civilization in the Malayan Archipelago.

Malaysia's Hindu Heritage:

In Malaysia, Hindu influences have endured through the ages. The ancient state of Kedah, known as Kadaram in historical texts, bore witness to Hindu-Buddhist influence. The Bujang Valley, with its archaeological remnants, attests to a thriving civilization engaged in trade, agriculture, and cultural exchanges. Hinduism's footprints can still be seen in the Batu Caves, where the iconic limestone caves host a vibrant annual Thaipusam festival.

Cultural Syncretism:

The enduring legacy of Hindu influences in the Malayan Archipelago is characterized by cultural syncretism. Local animistic beliefs, indigenous practices, and Hindu traditions interwove to create unique expressions of spirituality. The incorporation of Hindu deities, rituals, and festivals into local customs reflects a harmonious blending that defines the cultural ethos of the region.

Influence on Arts and Literature:

Hindu influences resonate through the arts and literature of the Malayan Archipelago. Wayang kulit, the traditional shadow puppetry in Indonesia and Malaysia, often draws inspiration from Hindu epics like the Ramayana and Mahabharata. Traditional dances, such as the Balinese Legong, bear traces of Hindu mythological narratives, enriching the performing arts of the region.

Temple Architecture:

The architectural landscape of the Malayan Archipelago is adorned with Hindu temples that stand as testaments to the enduring cultural exchanges. The Prambanan Temple complex in Indonesia, dedicated to the Trimurti, and the majestic Angkor Wat in Cambodia, influenced by Hindu cosmology, showcase the architectural splendor inspired by Hindu ideologies.

Challenges and Preservation:

While the influence of Hinduism in the Malayan Archipelago has persisted, it has also faced challenges. The ebb and flow of political dynamics, religious shifts, and external influences have impacted the preservation of this cultural heritage. Efforts to safeguard and revive Hindu traditions, however, underscore the resilience of communities in maintaining their cultural roots.

Modern Reflections:

In contemporary Malaysia, Hinduism remains a vibrant component of the nation's cultural diversity. Thaipusam, Deepavali, and other Hindu festivals are celebrated with enthusiasm, reflecting the continued relevance of Hindu traditions in the lives of Malaysians. The multicultural ethos of Malaysia, with its diverse religious practices, is a testament to the enduring impact of historical Hindu influences.

The Malayan Archipelago stands as a testament to the intricate dance of cultures, where Hindu influences have melded with indigenous traditions, shaping a rich and diverse heritage. This exploration into the historical currents and cultural legacies invites us to appreciate the profound impact of Hinduism in Malaysia and beyond—a cultural symphony that echoes through time, resonating in the vibrant landscapes of the Malayan Archipelago.

Philippines and Beyond: Island Chains as Hubs of Hindu Thought

In the vast expanse of the Philippine archipelago and neighboring island chains, where the Pacific Ocean whispers tales of ancient voyages, a compelling narrative unfolds—a story of vibrant cultural exchanges and the profound influence of Hindu thought. This exploration delves into the historical crosscurrents that have shaped the spiritual tapestry of these islands, transcending geographical boundaries and fostering a unique fusion of indigenous cultures with the rich philosophical traditions of Hinduism.

Maritime Trade Routes:

The Philippines, situated strategically along ancient maritime trade routes, became a hub for cultural exchanges. Traders, seafarers, and settlers navigated these waters, carrying not only goods but also the intangible wealth of Hindu ideas, beliefs, and practices. The archipelago served as a meeting point, where diverse cultures intermingled, giving rise to a syncretic blend that enriched the spiritual landscape.

Lingering Hindu Influences:

The echoes of Hindu thought resonate in the linguistic, artistic, and religious facets of the Philippines. Linguistic traces, such as loanwords and ancient scripts, hint at the historical connections with Hindu cultures.

The Maranao people, for instance, preserve ancient epics and stories that draw inspiration from Hindu mythology, contributing to the cultural continuity.

Archaeological Discoveries:

Archaeological excavations reveal the vestiges of a bygone era, where Hindu-Buddhist influences left their mark. The Butuan Ivory Seal, an artifact discovered in the Philippines, bears script reminiscent of ancient Indian characters, providing tangible evidence of historical connections. Lingering remnants of temples and artifacts affirm the once vibrant presence of Hindu thought.

Cultural Syncretism:

The Philippines and neighboring island chains exemplify a harmonious fusion of

Hindu ideas with indigenous belief systems. Mythologies, rituals, and cosmological concepts seamlessly interweaved, creating a unique tapestry where Anito spirits and Hindu deities coexist in the spiritual consciousness of local communities.

Philippine Deities and Rituals:

Hindu deities found a place of reverence in the pantheon of Philippine spirits. Lakanday, the god of hunters and warriors, shares similarities with Hindu deities like Shiva. Ancestor worship, a prominent aspect of Philippine spirituality, echoes Hindu concepts of reverence for forebears and a cosmic connection between the living and the departed.

Maharlika and Social Structure:

The concept of Maharlika, denoting a noble

class in ancient Philippine societies, reflects an influence from Indian societal structures. The notion of a hierarchical social order, reminiscent of the Varna system, suggests a cultural interplay that shaped not only spiritual beliefs but also societal norms.

Influence on Arts and Crafts:

The artistic expressions of the Philippines bear the imprint of Hindu thought. Traditional dances, like the Singkil, draw inspiration from Hindu epics, and intricate craftsmanship in jewelry and textiles reflects the influence of Hindu aesthetics. The Garuda, a mythical bird in Hindu mythology, finds its counterpart in Philippine folklore.

Challenges and Preservation:

The preservation of Hindu influences in the

Philippines faces challenges, including the passage of time, changing cultural landscapes, and the impact of external forces. Efforts to document, revive, and celebrate these influences underscore the importance of recognizing and safeguarding the cultural heritage embedded in the archipelago's history.

Modern Reflections:

In contemporary times, the legacy of Hindu thought in the Philippines continues to be a source of cultural richness. While the archipelago is predominantly Christianized, the cultural syncretism forged over centuries endures in festivals, linguistic elements, and artistic expressions, reflecting a living connection to the historical intersections with Hindu cultures.

The Philippines and neighboring island chains emerge as fascinating hubs of Hindu thought, where historical currents have shaped a diverse and resilient cultural landscape. This exploration invites us to contemplate the enduring impact of Hinduism on these distant shores—a testament to the interconnectedness of civilizations across the vast expanses of the Pacific and the enduring legacy of spiritual wisdom that transcends time and tides.

Chapter 8: Persian Connections

In the ancient tapestry of cultural interplay, where empires rose and fell, the narrative of Persian Connections unfolds—a captivating exploration into the historical threads that bound the realms of Hinduism and Zoroastrianism. Against the backdrop of shifting sands and ancient trade routes, the Persian influence on Hindu thought and vice versa created a complex and fascinating web of spiritual, philosophical, and artistic exchanges.

This journey delves into the corridors of time where the empires of Persia and the Indian subcontinent engaged in cultural dialogues. From the Achaemenids to the

Sassanids, the Zoroastrian flame flickered in tandem with the sacred fires of Hindu rituals. This exploration seeks to unravel the subtle connections, shared mythologies, and cross-fertilization of ideas that characterized the entwined destinies of these two ancient civilizations. Join us on a quest to trace the echoes of ancient chants, the whispers of shared wisdom, and the cultural dance that unfolded in the meeting grounds of Persia and the Indian subcontinent—a testament to the enduring dialogue that shaped the spiritual landscapes of both regions.

Avesta and Vedas: Interweaving Zoroastrianism and Hinduism

In the historical tapestry of religious and cultural exchanges, the interplay between Zoroastrianism and Hinduism emerges as a captivating narrative—a story of shared wisdom, intertwined destinies, and the subtle dance of spiritual syncretism. This exploration delves into the intricate patterns woven by the ancient adherents of Zoroastrianism and Hinduism, revealing a rich tapestry of interconnected beliefs, rituals, and philosophical currents that unfolded across the vast landscapes of Persia and the Indian subcontinent.

Shared Mythologies and Cosmic Concepts:

At the heart of the interweaving of Zoroastrianism and Hinduism lies a shared repository of mythologies and cosmic concepts. The ancient Indo-Iranian cultural exchanges manifested in similarities between Vedic and Zoroastrian deities, such as Mitra and Mithra, and the parallel concepts of cosmic dualism—the struggle between forces of light and darkness.

Fire Worship and Ritual Practices:

Both Zoroastrianism and Hinduism exhibit a profound reverence for fire as a sacred symbol of purity and divinity. The Zoroastrian Atash Behram and the Hindu Agni share a common thread of fire worship, reflecting a shared understanding of the transformative and purifying power inherent in this element.

Philosophical Parallels:

The philosophical underpinnings of Zoroastrianism and Hinduism reveal intriguing parallels. Zoroastrianism's emphasis on ethical dualism, with the eternal struggle between Ahura Mazda and Angra Mainyu, finds resonance with Hindu concepts of dharma and karma. The pursuit of righteous living and the cosmic balance are threads that intricately connect the spiritual philosophies of both traditions.

Solar and Cosmic Symbolism:

Solar symbolism, representing the journey of the sun across the sky, features prominently in both Zoroastrian and Hindu iconography. The reverence for the sun as a symbol of cosmic order and divine illumination is evident in Zoroastrian rituals and Hindu hymns, underscoring a shared appreciation for celestial forces.

Cultural Crosscurrents in Ancient Empires:

The historical interactions between the Persian Achaemenid and Sassanid Empires and the Indian subcontinent fostered cultural crosscurrents that left an indelible mark on both Zoroastrianism and Hinduism. The exchange of knowledge, artistic expressions, and administrative practices enriched the spiritual and cultural landscapes of these ancient civilizations.

Trade Routes and Diaspora Communities:

The Silk Road and other ancient trade routes facilitated not only the exchange of goods but also the dissemination of religious and cultural ideas. Diaspora communities, residing in regions influenced by both Zoroastrian and Hindu traditions, became conduits for the interweaving of beliefs, resulting in syncretic practices that endured through generations.

Challenges and Preservation:

Despite the interweaving of Zoroastrianism and Hinduism, each tradition faced challenges to its preservation. External influences, invasions, and the passage of time contributed to the evolution and, at times, the decline of certain aspects of these ancient faiths. However, the resilience of adherents and preservation efforts highlight the enduring value placed on these intertwined threads of wisdom.

Modern Echoes:

In contemporary times, echoes of the interweaving of Zoroastrianism and Hinduism can still be discerned. From shared cultural practices to the recognition of common symbols, the legacy of ancient exchanges continues to reverberate in the spiritual consciousness of communities influenced by these two venerable traditions.

The interweaving of Zoroastrianism and Hinduism emerges as a nuanced dance of shared insights, cultural exchanges, and mutual influences. This exploration invites us to appreciate the intricate patterns woven by the adherents of these ancient faiths, illuminating a shared journey of spiritual exploration that transcends temporal and geographical boundaries.

Persian Gulf Dynamics: Trade and Cultural Exchange in Ancient Persia

In the vast expanse of ancient Persia, where empires flourished along the crossroads of the East and West, a dynamic interplay of trade and cultural exchange unfolded—a tapestry woven with threads of silk, spices, and shared wisdom. This exploration delves into the vibrant landscapes of the Persian Empire, tracing the intricate routes of commerce and the flourishing cross-cultural connections that shaped the destiny of this ancient realm.

Silk Road and Beyond:

At the heart of Persian trade and cultural exchange lay the legendary Silk Road—a network of interconnected trade routes that spanned from the Mediterranean to China. Persian merchants, known for their commercial acumen, played a pivotal role as intermediaries in this transcontinental exchange, facilitating the flow of goods, ideas, and cultural influences.

Bazaars and Caravanserais:

Persian cities were adorned with bustling bazaars, vibrant marketplaces where traders from distant lands converged. Caravanserais, strategically positioned along trade routes, provided havens for merchants and travelers, fostering not only economic transactions but also the exchange of diverse cultural practices, languages, and artistic expressions.

Cultural Diversity in the Persian Empire:

The expansive nature of the Persian Empire—from the Mediterranean to the Indus River—contributed to a melting pot of cultures. The Achaemenid rulers embraced a policy of tolerance, allowing the coexistence of various ethnicities, religions, and traditions. This cultural diversity became a hallmark of the empire, creating a rich tapestry of artistic, linguistic, and religious syncretism.

Luxuries and Commodities:

Persian trade routes were conduits for a plethora of goods, transforming the empire into a hub of luxury and opulence. Precious spices, textiles, gemstones, and exotic animals traversed the vast expanses, enriching the material and cultural landscapes of Persia. The demand for such commodities spurred economic prosperity and cultural diffusion.

Zoroastrianism and Cultural Diffusion:

As the spiritual heart of the Persian Empire, Zoroastrianism played a role in cultural diffusion. The Zoroastrian fire temples, centers of worship and intellectual exchange, became focal points where not only religious ideas but also scientific and philosophical knowledge flowed between East and West. Zoroastrianism itself absorbed influences from neighboring cultures, contributing to a broader cultural synthesis.

Artistic and Architectural Synthesis:

Persian art and architecture reflected the amalgamation of diverse cultural influences. The monumental Persepolis, a testament to Achaemenid grandeur, showcased artistic motifs inspired by Egyptian, Mesopotamian, and Greek aesthetics. This synthesis extended to the intricate tilework, textiles, and metalwork, where Persian artisans blended local traditions with those imported through trade.

Educational and Intellectual Centers:

Cities like Persepolis and Susa emerged as intellectual hubs, attracting scholars, philosophers, and scientists from various corners of the empire and beyond. The Royal Road, a remarkable feat of engineering, facilitated swift communication and travel, fostering the exchange of ideas that contributed to the intellectual flourishing of the Persian Empire.

Decline and Legacy:

The decline of the Persian Empire, marked by invasions and shifts in political power, did not erase its legacy of trade and cultural exchange. The conquests of Alexander the Great and subsequent empires continued to build upon the foundations laid by the Achaemenids, perpetuating the interconnectedness of East and West.

Modern Reflections:

In modern times, the echoes of ancient Persian trade and cultural exchange reverberate. The enduring legacy can be seen in the linguistic influences, culinary traditions, and architectural motifs that have transcended centuries, testifying to the enduring impact of this dynamic interplay on the cultural heritage of the regions that were once part of the Persian Empire.

The tale of trade and cultural exchange in ancient Persia unfolds as a testament to the transformative power of commerce and shared ideas. This exploration invites us to traverse the ancient caravan routes, where merchants and intellectuals alike wove a tapestry of cultural richness—a legacy that endures in the global interconnections of today.

Sassanian Synthesis: Mutual Influences in Ancient Persia

In the realm of ancient Persia, the Sassanian Empire stands as a beacon of cultural synthesis—a flourishing epoch where mutual influences between indigenous traditions and external elements shaped a distinctive tapestry of art, religion, and governance. This exploration delves into the Sassanian synthesis, unraveling the intricate threads of influence that wove together a unique Persian identity during this transformative era.

Zoroastrian Revival:

The Sassanian rulers embarked on a deliberate revival of Zoroastrianism, elevating it to the status of the empire's official religion. The Avesta, the sacred scripture of Zoroastrianism, was compiled and codified during this period, fostering a cultural and religious renaissance that permeated various facets of Sassanian society.

Architectural Marvels:

Sassanian architecture exemplified a synthesis of indigenous Iranian elements with influences from neighboring civilizations. The iconic Taq Kasra, an expansive arch in Ctesiphon, showcased innovative engineering and design, blending Persian artistic motifs with Mesopotamian and Hellenistic influences. The use of intricate stucco reliefs and grandiose structures reflected a synthesis of diverse architectural styles.

Cultural Crossroads:

Situated at the crossroads of major trade routes, the Sassanian Empire became a melting pot of diverse cultures. The thriving cities of Persepolis, Ctesiphon, and Istakhr became centers of cultural exchange, where Persian, Mesopotamian, Indian, and Central Asian influences mingled, contributing to a rich and cosmopolitan society.

Influence of Silk Road:

The Silk Road, a major trade route

connecting the East and West, facilitated the exchange of goods, ideas, and artistic styles. Sassanian Persia, as a key player along this trade route, witnessed the influx of silk, spices, and philosophical concepts. The adoption of new artistic techniques and the assimilation of foreign cultural elements became integral to the Sassanian ethos.

Artistic Syncretism:

Sassanian art exemplified a syncretic blend of diverse influences. Intricate metalwork, vibrant textiles, and rock reliefs showcased a fusion of Persian, Roman, and Central Asian artistic elements. Royal imagery, including the iconic Sassanian crown, demonstrated an amalgamation of indigenous symbols with those borrowed from neighboring cultures.

Literary Contributions:

The Sassanian period witnessed notable contributions to Persian literature. Works like the "Book of Kings" (Shahnameh) by Ferdowsi drew inspiration from both pre-Islamic Persian epics and the cultural reservoir of neighboring civilizations. This literary synthesis played a crucial role in preserving and transmitting Persian cultural identity through the ages.

Religious Tolerance and Diverse Beliefs:

While Zoroastrianism was the state religion, the Sassanian Empire exhibited religious tolerance. Communities adhering to Christianity, Judaism, and other faiths coexisted within its borders. This pluralistic approach contributed to a mosaic of religious beliefs, fostering intellectual exchange and the cohabitation of diverse spiritual traditions.

Scientific and Medical Advancements:

Sassanian Persia made significant strides in scientific and medical knowledge. The Academy of Gondishapur, a renowned center of learning, became a melting pot for scholars from various backgrounds. Greek, Indian, and Persian contributions converged, leading to advancements in medicine, astronomy, and philosophy.

Decline and Legacy:

The Sassanian Empire faced challenges from external forces, particularly the Arab conquests in the 7th century. Despite its decline, the Sassanian synthesis left an enduring legacy. The cultural fusion and innovations of this period laid the groundwork for the subsequent Islamic Golden Age, as Persian scholars and traditions continued to shape the intellectual landscape.

Modern Reflections:

The Sassanian synthesis echoes in modern Iranian identity. Elements of Sassanian art, literature, and architecture persist in contemporary Iran, underscoring the enduring impact of this vibrant era on the cultural heritage of the region.

The Sassanian synthesis stands as a testament to the dynamic interplay of cultures and ideas, forging a distinctive Persian identity that transcended borders and epochs. This exploration invites us to appreciate the richness of a bygone era, where mutual influences became the building blocks of a cultural legacy that continues to resonate in the annals of Persian history.

Chapter 9: Mediterranean Mosaics

The sun-drenched shores of the Mediterranean have long been a theater of human drama—a stage upon which countless civilizations played out their tales of conquest, collaboration, and cultural exchange. In the mosaic of histories that adorn these ancient lands, we find threads woven by Phoenician traders, Greek philosophers, Roman conquerors, and a myriad of diverse cultures converging along the sea's expansive horizons.

This exploration beckons us to traverse the landscapes where ancient ports buzzed with the commerce of goods and ideas. From the

Iberian Peninsula to the Anatolian coast, the Mediterranean witnessed the rise and fall of empires, each contributing a tessera to the mosaic that defines the region's rich heritage. Echoes of diverse languages, religious beliefs, and artistic expressions resound in the ruins of once-mighty cities and the remnants of ancient harbors.

As we navigate through the archaeological sites and delve into the literary remnants of the past, we uncover the subtle interplay of cultures—a cultural intermingling that fostered intellectual enlightenment, technological innovation, and artistic brilliance. The Mediterranean, as a crucible of civilization, forged connections that transcended geographical boundaries, leaving an enduring legacy in the intricate patterns of human history. This journey invites us to witness the vibrancy of ancient interactions, to decipher the nuances of cultural syncretism, and to appreciate the mosaic of influences that have shaped the timeless allure of the Mediterranean world.

Hellenistic Harmonies: Hinduism's Encounters with Greek Civilization

In the annals of ancient history, the convergence of Hinduism and Greek civilization stands as a fascinating chapter—a meeting of two great cultural streams that flowed across distant lands, finding points of intersection and exchange. This exploration takes us on a journey through time, where the sacred rivers of Hindu thought encounter the philosophical currents of the Greeks, weaving a tapestry of intellectual dialogues, artistic expressions, and shared contemplations.

Geographical and Temporal Proximity:

While separated by vast geographical expanses, the Hellenistic world and the Indian subcontinent shared a temporal proximity during the 4th to 2nd centuries BCE. The campaigns of Alexander the Great brought Greek influence to the doorstep of the Indian subcontinent, creating a unique crucible where the legacy of Alexander's conquests intersected with the flourishing realms of ancient Indian civilization.

Syncretism in Gandhara Art:

The Gandhara region, at the crossroads of Central Asia and the Indian subcontinent, became a melting pot where Hellenistic and Indian artistic traditions fused. The Gandhara school of art produced sculptures that harmoniously blended Greek aesthetic elements with the iconographic conventions of Hindu and Buddhist traditions. Greek deities, such as Herakles, found sculptural expression alongside Bodhisattvas and Hindu divinities, reflecting a syncretic artistic synthesis.

Philosophical Dialogues:

The philosophical currents of the Greeks, particularly the inquiries of the Stoics and Pyrrhonists, found resonance in certain strands of Hindu thought. Both traditions grappled with questions of existence, ethics, and the nature of reality. The Upanishadic exploration of the self (Atman) and the Greek pursuit of eudaimonia, or flourishing, reveal parallels in the quest for higher truths.

Epic Narratives and Mythology:

The epic narratives of Hinduism, particularly the Mahabharata and Ramayana, share intriguing parallels with Greek mythology. The hero's journey, the concept of fate, and the interplay between gods and mortals resonate across traditions. Notable connections include the parallels between the Greek hero Herakles and the divine hero Krishna, both embodying a synthesis of human and divine attributes.

Scientific and Astronomical Exchanges:

In the realm of science and astronomy, exchanges occurred between Greek and Indian scholars. The transmission of mathematical knowledge, particularly geometry, is evidenced in texts such as the "Yavanajataka," an Indian astronomical treatise that incorporates Greek mathematical concepts. This cross-cultural fertilization contributed to advancements in both Hellenistic and Indian scientific thought.

Diplomatic Relations:

Historical accounts suggest diplomatic interactions between Hellenistic and Indian rulers. The Mauryan Emperor Chandragupta, for instance, is said to have received Hellenistic envoys and maintained contact with the Seleucid Empire. These interactions extended beyond military alliances to cultural exchanges, fostering a climate of mutual curiosity and understanding.

Buddhism as a Bridge:

The spread of Buddhism served as a cultural bridge between Hellenistic and Indian worlds. As the teachings of the Buddha traveled along trade routes, Greek-speaking communities in Central Asia became exposed to Buddhist thought. This intersection further facilitated the flow of cultural ideas, influencing artistic representations and philosophical discussions in both traditions.

Legacy in Western Indology:

The encounters between Hinduism and Greek civilization left a lasting impact on Western Indology. The study of Sanskrit texts by European scholars in the 18th and 19th centuries, particularly the works of Sir William Jones, reflected an intellectual curiosity inspired by the perceived connections between Greek and Indian languages and cultures.

Hinduism's encounters with Greek civilization embody a nuanced interplay of diverse cultures, sparking intellectual dialogues and artistic cross-pollination. This exploration invites us to appreciate the dynamic intersections that occurred at the crossroads of ancient horizons, enriching both Hellenistic and Indian civilizations with the enduring legacy of mutual influence.

Indo-Greek Kingdoms: Cross-Cultural Influences in Bactria and Beyond

The Indo-Greek Kingdoms, flourishing at the confluence of the Indian subcontinent and the Hellenistic world, stand as a testament to the extraordinary cross-cultural exchanges that unfolded in the heart of Bactria and its neighboring regions. This exploration unveils the dynamic interplay of influences that characterized the Indo-Greek Kingdoms, fostering a fusion of Hellenistic and Indian traditions in realms ranging from art and religion to governance and societal norms.

Historical Genesis:

The establishment of the Indo-Greek Kingdoms traced its roots to the campaigns of Alexander the Great and the subsequent fragmentation of his empire. Bactria, a region encompassing parts of modern-day Afghanistan and Central Asia, became a crucible where Greek and Indian cultural currents converged, giving rise to a series of Hellenistic-influenced kingdoms.

Syncretic Artistic Expressions:

One of the defining features of the Indo-Greek Kingdoms was the syncretism evident in artistic expressions. The Gandhara school of art, centered in the region of present-day Pakistan and Afghanistan, epitomized this fusion. Sculptures depicted Buddha and Bodhisattvas with distinct Hellenistic features, illustrating the harmonious blend of Greek and Indian artistic traditions.

Cultural Exchange in Religion:

Religious syncretism flourished in the Indo-Greek Kingdoms, with Greek and Indian deities often depicted together. Coins minted by Indo-Greek rulers featured representations of Greek gods, such as Zeus and Herakles, alongside images of Hindu deities like Shiva and Vishnu. This blending of religious iconography attested to a shared spiritual landscape.

Governing Practices and Administration:

The Indo-Greek rulers adopted a pragmatic approach to governance that combined elements of Greek administrative structures with local Indian practices. Inscriptions and coins from the period reveal bilingual usage of Greek and Prakrit languages, emphasizing the rulers' recognition of the diverse linguistic and cultural landscape of their domains.

Coinage and Cultural Symbols:

The coinage of the Indo-Greek Kingdoms served as a canvas for cultural synthesis. Coins featured bilingual inscriptions, often bearing the names of rulers in both Greek and Brahmi scripts. Additionally, the use of cultural symbols, such as the depiction of elephant-mounted gods and Greek deities, underscored the coexistence of diverse cultural identities.

Urban Centers and Trade Hubs:

Urban centers like Taxila and Ai-Khanoum became vibrant hubs where diverse cultural influences intermingled. These cities thrived as centers of commerce, scholarship, and artistic production. The agora-style marketplaces, architectural designs, and cultural practices mirrored the amalgamation of Greek and Indian lifestyles.

Scientific and Intellectual Exchanges:

The Indo-Greek Kingdoms were not only conduits for artistic and religious exchanges but also centers for intellectual pursuits. Scholars and philosophers from both Greek and Indian traditions engaged in a dialogue that contributed to advancements in fields such as astronomy, medicine, and philosophy. This intellectual cross-pollination enriched the intellectual fabric of the region.

Military Alliances and Conflicts:

The Indo-Greek Kingdoms navigated a complex geopolitical landscape marked by military alliances and conflicts. Rulers like Menander I engaged in military campaigns, forging alliances with local Indian rulers while occasionally clashing with neighboring powers. These interactions influenced the dynamics of power and cultural exchange in the region.

Legacy and Aftermath:

The Indo-Greek Kingdoms left a lasting legacy that reverberated beyond their decline. The cultural syncretism witnessed during this period contributed to the enduring cross-cultural influences in the region. The subsequent empires that rose in Bactria, such as the Kushan Empire, inherited and further developed the amalgamation of Hellenistic and Indian traditions.

The Indo-Greek Kingdoms emerge as a remarkable chapter in the tapestry of ancient history, illustrating the dynamic interplay between Greek and Indian civilizations. This exploration invites us to traverse the diverse landscapes of Bactria and its surrounding regions, where the echoes of cross-cultural influences continue to resonate in the rich heritage of the Indian subcontinent.

Alexandria and Beyond: Hindu Philosophies in the Mediterranean Basin

In the wake of Alexander the Great's expansive conquests, a remarkable chapter of cultural exchange unfolded in the heart of the Mediterranean Basin, particularly in the vibrant city of Alexandria. This exploration delves into the intriguing interplay between Hindu philosophies and the intellectual milieu of the Mediterranean, unraveling the threads that connected the ancient wisdom of the Indian subcontinent with the philosophical tapestry of the Hellenistic world.

Formation of the Alexandrian School:

The establishment of the Alexandrian School became a crucible for intellectual crosscurrents. Scholars, philosophers, and mystics from diverse backgrounds converged, creating an environment where Greek philosophical traditions encountered the profound insights of Hindu thought. The Library of Alexandria, a beacon of knowledge, played a pivotal role in fostering this cross-cultural dialogue.

Transmission of Hindu Texts:

The influx of Hindu philosophical texts into Alexandria marked a significant turning point. Manuscripts containing foundational Hindu scriptures, including portions of the Vedas, Upanishads, and philosophical treatises, found their way into the hands of scholars eager to explore the mystical and metaphysical dimensions of Eastern thought.

Philosophical Synthesis:

The Alexandrian philosophers, influenced by the richness of Hindu philosophies, engaged in a process of synthesis. The concept of Brahman, the ultimate reality in Hinduism, resonated with the Neoplatonic ideas of the One. This synthesis gave rise to a harmonious blending of metaphysical principles, fostering a unique intellectual landscape in which Eastern and Western philosophies coexisted.

Mystical Dimensions and Meditation Practices:

Hindu contemplative practices, particularly those related to meditation and introspection, found resonance among the philosophers of Alexandria. The pursuit of mystical experiences, akin to the Hindu concept of self-realization, became a shared endeavor. The teachings of Hindu sages, such as those found in the Upanishads, provided a roadmap for exploring the depths of consciousness.

Cultural Crosscurrents in Alexandria:

The cosmopolitan nature of Alexandria, with its diverse population and thriving trade routes, created a melting pot of cultures. The city became a meeting ground for individuals from India, Persia, Greece, and beyond. The exchange of ideas, religious practices, and cultural expressions flourished, fostering an atmosphere of intellectual curiosity and mutual enrichment.

Hermeticism and Esoteric Traditions:

The Hermetic tradition, with its emphasis on spiritual transformation and the unity of the divine, drew inspiration from Hindu esoteric practices. The Hermetic writings, attributed to Hermes Trismegistus, echoed themes reminiscent of Hindu mysticism, contributing to the development of a mystical and esoteric strain within the broader philosophical discourse of Alexandria.

Architectural Synthesis and Temples of Serapis:

The architectural landscape of Alexandria mirrored the synthesis of cultures. The Serapeum, a temple dedicated to the god Serapis, embodied this fusion. The temple incorporated elements of both Greek and Egyptian religious traditions, reflecting the inclusive spirit of cultural amalgamation that defined the city.

Decline and Legacy:

The decline of the Alexandrian School was gradual, influenced by changing political landscapes and religious shifts. However, its legacy endured. The intellectual currents initiated by the engagement with Hindu philosophies persisted in various forms, influencing later philosophical movements and contributing to the broader understanding of mysticism and metaphysics.

Modern Reflections:

The echoes of the encounter between Hindu philosophies and the intellectual milieu of Alexandria resonate in modern discussions on comparative religion, mysticism, and the synthesis of diverse philosophical traditions. Scholars continue to explore the intersections between Eastern and Western thought, tracing the enduring legacy of this ancient cross-cultural dialogue.

The exploration of Hindu philosophies in the Mediterranean Basin, centered around Alexandria, invites us to appreciate the dynamic interplay of ideas that transcended geographical and cultural boundaries. This unique chapter in the history of philosophical exchange illustrates the enriching dialogue that occurred when the wisdom of the East met the intellectual currents of the Hellenistic world.

Chapter 10: European Echoes

In the intricate tapestry of religious and cultural exchanges, Hinduism's influence reverberates far beyond its geographical origins, reaching the heart of Europe. This exploration delves into the multifaceted ways in which Hindu ideas, practices, and philosophies have left an indelible mark on the European intellectual and cultural landscape.

From the early encounters between Indian and European civilizations to the philosophical dialogues that unfolded during the colonial era, the echoes of Hindu thought permeated European consciousness. We navigate through the intellectual salons, artistic expressions, and scholarly pursuits that bear the imprints of Hinduism. This investigation invites us to witness the enduring resonance of Hindu ideas, not merely as exotic imports, but as catalysts for transformative intellectual and cultural currents that have shaped Europe's understanding of spirituality, philosophy, and the interconnectedness of human experience. As we traverse this historical and philosophical landscape, This exploration unfolds as a testament to the enduring dialogue between two rich traditions, forging a shared narrative that transcends continental boundaries.

Roman Encounters: Hinduism in the Eyes of Ancient Europe

In the expansive tapestry of ancient history, the Roman Empire emerges as a focal point where diverse cultures converged, and ideas from distant lands found their way to the heart of Europe. Among these exotic influences, Hinduism, with its profound spiritual traditions and philosophical depth, made an indelible impact on the Roman consciousness. This exploration delves into the nuanced interactions between Rome and Hinduism, unraveling the threads of cultural exchange, intellectual curiosity, and the ways in which the ancient Romans perceived the profound beliefs emanating from the Indian subcontinent.

Trade Routes and Cultural Conduits:

As the Roman Empire expanded its dominion across the Mediterranean and beyond, trade routes became conduits for the exchange of goods and ideas. The Silk Road and maritime routes facilitated encounters between Roman merchants and the rich tapestry of Indian culture. Along with exotic spices and precious silks, Hindu philosophical ideas began to weave their way into the fabric of Roman society.

Philosophical Dialogues and Mystical Allure:

The intellectual milieu of ancient Rome, marked by its penchant for philosophical inquiry, found itself intrigued by the mysticism and spiritual profundity of Hindu thought. Philosophers such as Plotinus, influenced by Eastern ideas, engaged in dialogues that contemplated the nature of the divine, the self, and the interconnectedness of all existence. The allure of Hindu mysticism captivated Roman thinkers, sparking a curiosity that transcended geographical boundaries.

Perceptions of Hindu Deities:

The encounter with Hindu deities left an imprint on the Roman imagination. The similarities and divergences between Roman and Hindu pantheons prompted reflections on the nature of divinity. While the Romans sought to assimilate deities from conquered lands into their own pantheon, the exotic allure of Hindu gods and goddesses sparked contemplation on the plurality and universality of divine forces.

Artistic Synthesis:

The artistic expressions of the Roman world began to reflect the synthesis of cultural influences. Roman art, infused with Hellenistic traditions, adapted elements of Hindu iconography and symbolism. The juxtaposition of classical Roman aesthetics with representations of Hindu deities in sculptures and mosaics underscored the eclectic nature of artistic synthesis during this period.

Philosophical Syncretism in Alexandria:

The cosmopolitan city of Alexandria, a hub of intellectual exchange within the Roman Empire, played a pivotal role in the intermingling of Roman and Hindu ideas. The Alexandrian School became a meeting ground for scholars from diverse backgrounds, fostering a climate of syncretism where Eastern and Western philosophies converged.

The Influence on Mystery Cults:

The mystery cults of the Roman world, characterized by secretive rituals and esoteric teachings, absorbed elements of Hindu mysticism. The quest for spiritual enlightenment and initiation ceremonies bore echoes of Eastern spiritual practices, contributing to the eclectic nature of Roman religious experiences.

Decline and Fragmented Legacy:

As the Roman Empire declined and gave way to the medieval era, the direct interactions with Hindu thought diminished. However, the traces of this encounter persisted in fragmented ways. The legacy of Roman encounters with Hinduism found subtle expressions in medieval European literature, art, and philosophical discussions.

Modern Rediscovery and Scholarship:

In more recent times, the scholarship of historians and archaeologists has brought to light the nuances of Roman encounters with Hinduism. Inscriptions, artifacts, and the reinterpretation of ancient texts have shed new light on the profound impact that Hindu ideas had on the intellectual landscape of ancient Rome.

The Roman encounters with Hinduism illuminate a captivating chapter in the annals of cultural exchange. As the ancient world witnessed the interweaving of diverse traditions, the echoes of Hindu thought resonated in the intellectual, artistic, and spiritual pursuits of the Romans, leaving an enduring imprint on the multifaceted tapestry of ancient Europe.

Silk Routes to the West: The Diffusion of Hindu Ideas in the Roman Empire

The Silk Routes, known as conduits of

commerce and cultural exchange, became vibrant channels through which Hindu ideas traversed from the Indian subcontinent to the heart of the Roman Empire. This exploration unveils the intricate tapestry of interactions, intellectual exchanges, and spiritual diffusion that characterized the dissemination of Hindu ideas along the Silk Routes to the West.

Trade and Cultural Confluence:

The Silk Routes facilitated not only the trade of goods but also the exchange of ideas between East and West. As Indian merchants traversed the overland and maritime routes, the rich tapestry of Hindu culture, philosophy, and spirituality unfolded before the eyes of those in the Roman Empire. The bustling marketplaces and cosmopolitan cities along these routes became crucibles of cultural confluence.

Perceptions in the Roman World:

The encounter with Hindu ideas sparked the curiosity of the Roman elite and intellectuals. Roman writers and historians, including Pliny the Elder and Strabo, documented the wonders of India, describing religious practices, philosophical concepts, and the opulence of Indian society. These accounts provided glimpses into the exotic and spiritual allure of Hinduism.

Syncretism in Art and Iconography:

The diffusion of Hindu ideas left an indelible mark on Roman art. The syncretic blending of artistic styles and iconography became evident in sculptures and reliefs that incorporated elements inspired by Hindu traditions. Images of deities with multiple arms and intricate motifs found their way into Roman artistic expressions.

Philosophical Dialogues:

The intellectual exchanges along the Silk Routes led to philosophical dialogues between Eastern and Western thinkers. Hindu metaphysical concepts, such as the interconnectedness of all things and the pursuit of spiritual enlightenment, resonated with certain schools of thought in the Roman world. This cross-pollination enriched the philosophical discourse in both cultures.

Influence on Roman Mysticism:

Hindu mysticism, with its emphasis on meditation, self-realization, and the pursuit of inner peace, influenced Roman mysticism and esoteric traditions. The appeal of Eastern mystique, coupled with the allure of spiritual practices, contributed to the development of a mystical strain within Roman philosophical circles.

Transmission of Texts:

The translation of Hindu philosophical texts into Greek and Latin played a crucial role in the diffusion of ideas. Manuscripts containing Upanishads, Vedas, and other sacred texts found their way into the hands of Roman scholars, opening a gateway to the profound wisdom encapsulated in Hindu scriptures.

Cultural Integration in Roman Religion:

While not leading to the wholesale adoption of Hindu religious practices, the diffusion of ideas did influence Roman religious syncretism. Elements of Hindu cosmology, symbolism, and religious concepts found echoes in certain Roman cults and mystical traditions.

Legacy in Roman Intellectual Heritage:

The diffusion of Hindu ideas along the Silk Routes left a lasting legacy in Roman intellectual heritage. The openness to diverse philosophies and the incorporation of Eastern elements contributed to the rich intellectual tapestry of the Roman Empire, shaping its worldview and cultural identity.

Transformation and Evolution:

As the Roman Empire faced political and social transformations, the dynamics of cultural diffusion evolved. The decline of the empire marked a shift in the nature of interactions with distant cultures, but the traces of Hindu influence persisted in various forms within the evolving European cultural landscape.

The Silk Routes to the West stand as a

testament to the dynamic diffusion of Hindu ideas into the Roman Empire. This exploration invites us to traverse the ancient trade routes, witnessing the interplay of cultures and the intellectual exchanges that enriched both Eastern and Western civilizations, leaving an enduring imprint on the tapestry of human history.

Cultural Migrations: Indian Influences on Greco-Roman Thought

In the corridors of antiquity, a profound cultural migration occurred as the ideas, philosophies, and spiritual traditions of India permeated the intellectual landscape of the Greco-Roman world. This exploration delves into the nuanced interactions, philosophical dialogues, and transformative exchanges that unfolded as Indian influences left an indelible mark on the thought systems of ancient Greece and Rome.

Early Contacts and the Edges of Empires:

The initial encounters between Indian and Greco-Roman cultures were facilitated by the expansive empires that bordered each other. As the Achaemenid Persian Empire served as a mediator, fostering connections between the Indian subcontinent and the Hellenistic world, cultural emissaries and traders embarked on journeys that would shape the course of intellectual history.

Philosophical Synthesis:

The convergence of Indian and Greco-Roman thought gave rise to a philosophical synthesis, with scholars engaging in dialogues that transcended cultural boundaries. The Indian concept of Dharma found parallels in Stoic philosophy, emphasizing ethical conduct and the cosmic order. This cross-fertilization enriched the philosophical tapestry, fostering a shared exploration of human existence.

Mysticism and the Quest for Inner Knowledge:

Indian mysticism, rooted in practices like meditation and self-realization, resonated with certain philosophical currents in the Greco-Roman world. The pursuit of inner knowledge and the contemplation of metaphysical truths became common ground, fostering a shared quest for spiritual enlightenment.

Influence on Neoplatonism:

The Neoplatonic school of thought, with luminaries such as Plotinus, drew inspiration from Indian metaphysical ideas. The concept of an ultimate reality beyond the material world, akin to the Indian notion of Brahman, influenced the Neoplatonic understanding of the One, a transcendent principle underlying all existence.

Esoteric Traditions and Mystery Cults:

The mystery cults of the Greco-Roman world, characterized by esoteric rituals and secret knowledge, exhibited traces of Indian influences. The notion of initiation, transformative experiences, and the pursuit of hidden truths mirrored certain elements of Indian spiritual practices, contributing to the mystique of these cults.

Transmission of Indian Texts:

The translation of Indian philosophical texts

into Greek and Latin played a pivotal role in the dissemination of Indian ideas. Manuscripts containing excerpts from the Vedas, Upanishads, and other sacred texts found their way into the hands of Greco-Roman scholars, providing a window into the profound insights of Indian wisdom.

Cultural Syncretism in Art and Iconography:

The artistic expressions of the Greco-Roman world reflected a syncretic blending of cultural motifs. Influences from Indian iconography, such as representations of deities with multiple arms, found their way into Roman art, creating a visual dialogue that transcended geographical and cultural divides.

Impact on Healing Practices:

The Indian understanding of holistic well-being and the interconnectedness of mind and body influenced healing practices in the Greco-Roman world. Aspects of Ayurveda and traditional Indian medicine found resonance in certain schools of thought, contributing to the development of holistic healing systems.

Legacy in Greco-Roman Intellectual Heritage:

The cultural migrations of Indian influences left an enduring legacy in the intellectual heritage of the Greco-Roman world. The openness to diverse philosophies and the incorporation of Indian elements contributed to the rich tapestry of thought that characterized this era.

Transformation and Evolution:

As the classical world transitioned through political, social, and cultural transformations, the legacy of Indian influences persisted in various forms. The echoes of these cultural migrations continued to resonate within the evolving intellectual landscape of Europe.

The cultural migrations of Indian influences on Greco-Roman thought stand as a testament to the profound interconnectedness of ancient civilizations. This exploration invites us to navigate through the crossroads of ideas, witnessing the transformative exchanges that shaped the intellectual heritage of both India and the Greco-Roman world, leaving an enduring imprint on the tapestry of human civilization.

Chapter 11: Oceania Odyssey

In the vast expanse of Oceania, where the Pacific Ocean unfurls its azure tapestry, an odyssey unfolds—a journey that transcends continents and weaves the threads of Hinduism into the cultural fabric of diverse island societies. This exploration invites us to embark on a captivating journey of discovery, unraveling the untold stories of spiritual migrations and cultural exchanges that have shaped the islands scattered across this expansive ocean.

From the ancient seafaring voyages that connected the Indian subcontinent to the distant shores of Oceania to the enduring influence of Hindu cosmology on indigenous belief systems, this odyssey traverses the waves of time, unveiling the subtle yet profound connections that have endured through centuries. As we navigate the islands, each with its unique traditions and mythologies, we encounter the echoes of Hindu epics, symbols, and philosophical concepts that have found a home amidst the palm-fringed beaches and lush landscapes.

This narrative beckons us to explore the confluence of spiritual currents, where the rhythms of the Pacific meld with the timeless essence of Hindu wisdom, creating a vibrant mosaic of cultural syncretism that defies geographical boundaries.

Polynesian Parallels: Traces of Hinduism in the Pacific Islands

In the vast and remote expanse of the Pacific Islands, far removed from the Indian subcontinent, subtle yet intriguing traces of Hinduism have left an indelible mark on the cultural landscapes of these isolated paradises. This exploration delves into the historical and archaeological evidence that unveils the presence of Hindu influences across the Pacific Islands, highlighting the interconnectedness of distant civilizations.

Seafaring Links:

The Pacific Islands, despite their geographical isolation, bear witness to the remarkable seafaring capabilities of ancient cultures. Evidence suggests that maritime routes connected the Indian subcontinent to these distant shores, fostering exchanges of not only goods but also ideas. The seafaring odysseys, reminiscent of Hindu maritime traditions, facilitated cultural currents that transcended vast oceanic expanses.

Mythological Parallels:

As we unravel the mythologies of the Pacific Islands, striking parallels with Hindu epics emerge. Stories of creation, deities, and cosmic battles bear uncanny resemblances to the narratives found in Hindu scriptures. The shared motifs of serpent symbolism and celestial beings hint at a cultural cross-pollination that defies the conventional boundaries of geography.

Sacred Sites and Temples:

Archaeological discoveries on certain Pacific

Islands reveal structures and artifacts reminiscent of Hindu temples. Intricately carved stones, resembling those used in Hindu temple architecture, suggest a deliberate effort to replicate sacred spaces. The alignment of these structures with celestial events mirrors Hindu astronomical principles, raising questions about the nature of cultural exchanges.

Symbolism and Rituals:

The use of Hindu symbols, such as the swastika, in Pacific Island cultures further underscores the permeation of Hindu influences. Ritual practices and ceremonies, including fire-walking and trance-inducing dances, bear resemblance to certain Hindu religious observances, hinting at shared spiritual elements that have endured through generations.

Philosophical Undercurrents:

Philosophical concepts found in Hinduism, such as the cyclical nature of time and the interconnectedness of all life, echo in the belief systems of some Pacific Island cultures. The reverence for nature and the recognition of a cosmic order align with Hindu notions of Dharma, suggesting a shared understanding of humanity's place in the larger tapestry of existence.

Trade and Cultural Exchange:

The trade networks that crisscrossed the Pacific Ocean served as conduits not only for material goods but also for the exchange of ideas. The presence of Hindu-influenced artifacts, including pottery and ornaments, suggests that these islands were integral nodes in a larger network of cultural exchange that spanned the vastness of the Pacific.

Integration and Adaptation:

Rather than a wholesale adoption of Hindu practices, the Pacific Islands showcase a unique process of integration and adaptation. Indigenous cultures absorbed elements of Hinduism into their own belief systems, weaving them seamlessly into the fabric of local traditions. This syncretism highlights the adaptability of Hindu ideas in diverse cultural settings.

Legacy and Continuity:

While the direct historical connections between the Indian subcontinent and the Pacific Islands may remain elusive, the legacy of Hindu influences persists. The shared symbols, mythologies, and spiritual concepts endure as a testament to the enduring impact of cultural interactions across the expansive canvas of the Pacific.

Traces of Hinduism in the Pacific Islands invites us to navigate the currents of history, uncovering the hidden connections that link the Indian subcontinent to the far reaches of the Pacific. This exploration challenges conventional narratives of cultural isolation, revealing a tapestry woven with threads of Hindu wisdom that have left their mark on the islands' cultures, creating a shared heritage that spans the vastness of the Pacific Ocean.

Maori Mysteries: Hindu Concepts in New Zealand's Indigenous Traditions

In the captivating landscapes of New Zealand, where the Maori people have cultivated a rich tapestry of indigenous traditions, echoes of Hindu concepts whisper through the winds and dance across the sacred terrains. This exploration delves into the nuanced interplay of spiritual ideas, mythologies, and cultural exchanges that have shaped the beliefs of the Maori, revealing the unexpected resonance with Hindu concepts in the heart of Aotearoa.

Mythological Parallels:

The cosmogonic myths of the Maori, with their intricate narratives of creation and ancestral beings, bear striking parallels to Hindu cosmology. The concept of Io, the supreme being in Maori mythology, shares similarities with the Hindu idea of a transcendental and formless ultimate reality. These mythological threads weave a narrative that transcends the geographical distances between the Indian subcontinent and the islands of New Zealand.

Sacred Geometry and Symbolism:

In Maori art and carvings, the use of sacred geometry and symbols reminiscent of Hindu iconography emerges as a fascinating convergence. Intricate patterns, spirals, and motifs mirroring the lotus flower, a symbol of divine purity in Hinduism, adorn Maori artworks. The presence of such shared symbols suggests a subtle yet profound cross-cultural dialogue.

Tapu and Sacredness:

The Maori concept of "tapu," signifying sacredness and restrictions on certain places or objects, bears resonance with the Hindu concept of the sacred and the profane. The reverence for certain spaces and rituals aligns with the Hindu understanding of the divine permeating all aspects of life, emphasizing the need for respect and ritual purity.

Ancestral Veneration and Reincarnation:

Both Maori and Hindu traditions emphasize the importance of ancestral veneration and the continuity of life beyond death. The Maori belief in the spiritual realm of Hawaiki, where ancestors reside, echoes the Hindu concept of reincarnation and the cycle of birth and rebirth. This shared understanding of the interconnectedness of past, present, and future forms a spiritual bridge between distant cultures.

Whakapapa and Lineage:

The Maori concept of "whakapapa," denoting genealogy and the interwoven connections between individuals and the land, mirrors the Hindu emphasis on lineage and the transmission of spiritual wisdom through familial ties. The idea that one's identity is intricately linked to their ancestors and the natural world resonates with the Hindu concept of Dharma, emphasizing one's duty within the cosmic order.

Nature Worship and Elemental Forces:

The Maori reverence for nature and the elemental forces finds resonance in Hindu traditions where the natural elements are considered manifestations of the divine. The sacredness attributed to mountains, rivers, and forests in Maori rituals aligns with the Hindu understanding of divinity inherent in the natural world.

Kapa Haka and Classical Dance:

The traditional Maori performing arts, known as "kapa haka," showcase rhythmic movements, facial expressions, and dynamic postures reminiscent of classical Indian dance forms. The parallels in the aesthetics of expression suggest a shared appreciation for the art of storytelling through bodily movements, transcending cultural boundaries.

Integration and Adaptation:

Rather than a wholesale adoption of Hindu concepts, the Maori tradition showcases a process of integration and adaptation. Indigenous beliefs and practices absorbed elements of Hindu wisdom, weaving them seamlessly into the cultural fabric. This syncretism illustrates the universality of certain spiritual concepts that can transcend cultural and geographical contexts.

Legacy and Contemporary Expressions:

The legacy of Hindu concepts in Maori traditions endures in contemporary expressions of art, spirituality, and rituals. As the Maori people continue to navigate the complexities of modernity, the subtle interweaving of Hindu influences persists, creating a dynamic cultural landscape that draws from diverse spiritual wellsprings.

the exploration of Hindu concepts within New Zealand's indigenous traditions unveils a rich tapestry of cultural interplay and spiritual resonance. The Maori people, with their deep-rooted traditions and profound connection to the land, embody a dynamic synthesis of indigenous wisdom and subtle Hindu influences. Through mythological parallels, sacred symbolism, ancestral veneration, and a shared reverence for nature, the spiritual dialogue between Hinduism and Maori culture transcends geographical boundaries and spans the depths of human experience.

As contemporary expressions of Maori identity continue to evolve, the legacy of Hindu concepts endures as a testament to the universality of spiritual truths and the resilience of cultural syncretism. In a world marked by diversity and interconnectedness, the exploration of shared spiritual heritage fosters understanding, dialogue, and appreciation for the multifaceted expressions of human spirituality. The journey through New Zealand's indigenous traditions invites us to embrace the interconnectedness of all cultures and to celebrate the rich tapestry of human experience that transcends borders and boundaries.

Australia's Aboriginal Affinities: Exploring Ancient Spiritual Connections

In the vast and ancient landscapes of Australia, the Aboriginal peoples have cultivated a profound spiritual heritage that resonates with the rhythms of the land and the cycles of nature. This exploration delves into the intricate web of spiritual connections that define Aboriginal cultures, uncovering the ancient affinities and subtle echoes of Hindu spiritual concepts that have shaped the spiritual landscape of the continent.

Dreamtime and Creation Myths:

Central to Aboriginal spirituality is the concept of the Dreamtime, a sacred era where ancestral beings shaped the landscape and imbued it with spiritual significance. Similar to Hindu cosmology, which speaks of cycles of creation and destruction, Dreamtime myths articulate the interconnectedness of all life and the timeless essence of existence.

Sacred Sites and Songlines:

Aboriginal spirituality is deeply intertwined with the land, and sacred sites hold immense spiritual significance as repositories of ancestral wisdom and power. The concept of Songlines, or Dreaming tracks, traces intricate pathways across the land, connecting sacred sites and encoding cultural knowledge through song, dance, and story. This profound connection to the land finds resonance with Hindu reverence for sacred geography and pilgrimage sites.

Animism and Totemism:

Aboriginal spiritual beliefs embrace animism, the belief that all living beings possess a spiritual essence and interconnectedness. The reverence for totem animals and ancestral spirits mirrors Hindu concepts of sacred animals and deities, emphasizing the interconnectedness of humans, animals, and the natural world.

Ceremonial Rituals and Dance:

Aboriginal ceremonial rituals, often characterized by dance, music, and storytelling, serve as pathways to connect with ancestral spirits and the Dreaming. The rhythmic movements and symbolic gestures found in Aboriginal dance traditions bear resemblance to the intricate mudras and expressions of devotion in Hindu classical dance forms, reflecting a shared understanding of the power of movement as a conduit for spiritual expression.

Cosmic Order and Balance:

Aboriginal spirituality emphasizes the importance of maintaining harmony and balance within the natural world, reflecting a deep respect for the interconnectedness of all living beings and the cycles of life. This reverence for the cosmic order resonates with Hindu concepts of Dharma, which underscores the universal principles of righteousness and duty that govern the universe.

Artistic Expressions and Symbolism:

Aboriginal art, with its intricate dot paintings, symbolic motifs, and storytelling traditions, serves as a visual testament to the spiritual richness of Aboriginal cultures.

The use of symbols and motifs reminiscent of Hindu iconography, such as the serpent and the lotus, suggests a subtle dialogue between distant spiritual traditions, transcending geographical and cultural boundaries.

Integration and Adaptation:

The interaction between Aboriginal and Hindu spiritual traditions illustrates a process of integration and adaptation, where diverse spiritual concepts find resonance and expression within local contexts. The syncretic blending of spiritual ideas reflects the resilience and adaptability of Aboriginal cultures in the face of cultural exchanges and historical transformations.

Legacy and Contemporary Expressions:

The legacy of Hindu spiritual concepts in

Aboriginal traditions endures in contemporary expressions of art, spirituality, and cultural revitalization. As Aboriginal communities navigate the complexities of modernity, the subtle interweaving of Hindu influences persists, enriching the spiritual tapestry of the continent and fostering a deeper appreciation for the interconnectedness of all cultures and spiritual traditions.

Australia's Aboriginal Affinities invite us to embark on a journey of spiritual exploration, traversing the landscapes of myth, symbolism, and ritual. This exploration illuminates the interconnectedness between Aboriginal spirituality and Hindu concepts, offering profound insights into the shared spiritual heritage that transcends borders and cultural divides. As we navigate the ancient spiritual connections of the continent, we

are reminded of the enduring power of
spiritual dialogue and the universal quest
for meaning and connection in the tapestry
of human experience.

Chapter 12: Diaspora Dynamics

In the vast tapestry of human history, the concept of Diaspora Dynamics emerges as a complex interplay of migration, cultural exchange, and the evolution of identities across geographical boundaries. From ancient civilizations to modern societies, the diaspora phenomenon embodies the resilience and adaptability of human communities in the face of displacement, dispersion, and interconnectedness.

At its core, Diaspora Dynamics encapsulates the multifaceted interactions between diasporic communities and their host societies, tracing the trajectories of cultural diffusion, hybridity, and adaptation that define the diasporic experience. Whether propelled by economic, political, or social forces, diaspora movements have shaped the contours of global history, leaving indelible imprints on the cultural landscapes of diverse regions.

The dynamics of diaspora are characterized by a myriad of factors, including the preservation of cultural heritage amidst assimilation, the negotiation of identities in transnational contexts, and the forging of new social networks across borders. These dynamics manifest in various forms, from the establishment of ethnic enclaves and cultural institutions to the emergence of transnational identities and virtual communities in the digital age.

Throughout history, diasporic communities have served as conduits of cultural exchange, innovation, and resilience, enriching host societies with their diverse traditions, languages, and perspectives. The diaspora experience embodies the human capacity for adaptation and transformation, offering a lens through which to understand the complexities of globalization, migration, and belonging in an increasingly interconnected world.

As we navigate the intricate web of Diaspora Dynamics, we embark on a journey of exploration and discovery, unraveling the threads of migration and belonging that weave through the fabric of human existence. This exploration invites us to engage with the rich tapestry of diasporic experiences, illuminating the enduring resilience and vibrant diversity of the human spirit across time and space.

Indian Diaspora: Hinduism in Migrant Communities

The diffusion of Hinduism across the globe has been significantly influenced by migration patterns, as adherents of the faith have ventured far beyond the Indian subcontinent, carrying their religious traditions and cultural practices to distant shores. The presence of Hinduism in migrant communities around the world underscores the adaptability and resilience of the religion, as well as its ability to evolve within diverse cultural contexts.

Cultural Retention and Adaptation:

In migrant communities, Hinduism often serves as a source of cultural identity and cohesion, fostering a sense of belonging and continuity amidst the challenges of adapting to new environments. For instance, Indian migrants in countries like the United States or the United Kingdom maintain their religious traditions through practices such as home worship, temple visits, and participation in religious festivals. However, the nature of Hinduism in migrant communities also reflects adaptations to local customs, languages, and social norms. In Trinidad and Tobago, Hindu traditions blend with Caribbean culture, resulting in unique expressions of the faith that resonate with the local population.

Community Cohesion and Social Networks:

Hindu temples and cultural centers play a pivotal role in migrant communities, serving as hubs for religious worship, social gatherings, and cultural events. These institutions provide a sense of community cohesion and support networks for migrants navigating the challenges of resettlement. For example, the Hindu temples in the Gulf countries not only cater to religious needs but also offer social services and networking opportunities for Indian expatriates, contributing to a sense of solidarity and community bonding.

Transnational Connections and Global Networks:

In an era of globalization, Hindu migrant communities maintain strong transnational connections with their homeland and with fellow Hindus around the world. Indian diaspora communities in countries like Canada or Australia actively engage in cultural exchanges and religious activities with their counterparts in India. Transnational Hindu organizations and online forums serve as platforms for dialogue, collaboration, and advocacy, fostering a sense of global solidarity among Hindus living abroad.

Interfaith Dialogue and Cultural Exchange:

Hindu migrant communities often engage in interfaith dialogue and cultural exchange initiatives with members of other religious and cultural groups in their host countries. These interactions promote mutual understanding, respect, and cooperation among diverse communities, contributing to social harmony and religious pluralism. In Fiji, for instance, Hindus actively participate in interfaith events and cultural festivals, fostering bonds of friendship and cooperation with neighbors of different faith traditions.

Challenges and Opportunities:

Despite the vibrancy and resilience of

Hinduism in migrant communities, challenges such as religious discrimination, cultural assimilation, and generational shifts pose significant concerns. In South Africa, for example, Hindu communities face challenges related to identity preservation amidst a diverse cultural landscape. However, these challenges also present opportunities for innovation, introspection, and community empowerment as Hindus navigate the complexities of identity, belonging, and cultural integration in their host countries.

The presence of Hinduism in migrant communities reflects the dynamic interplay between religious tradition and cultural adaptation, resilience and change, continuity and innovation. As Hindus around the world forge new pathways of migration and settlement, their religious practices and cultural expressions continue to evolve, enriching the tapestry of global Hinduism and contributing to the rich mosaic of religious diversity in migrant societies. Through collective efforts to preserve and celebrate their religious heritage, Hindus in migrant communities affirm their identity, strengthen their bonds of solidarity, and contribute to the vibrant tapestry of multiculturalism in their host countries.

African Diaspora: Hindu Traditions in the Global African Context

In the vast and diverse landscapes of Africa, the presence of Hindu traditions represents a fascinating intersection of cultures, histories, and spiritual expressions. As Hinduism has transcended geographical boundaries, it has found resonance and adaptation within the dynamic tapestry of

African societies, enriching local traditions and shaping the religious landscape in unexpected ways.

Historical Connections:

The historical connections between India and Africa date back centuries, marked by trade routes, cultural exchanges, and migrations. Indian merchants and sailors ventured to the eastern coast of Africa, establishing vibrant trading settlements and facilitating the exchange of goods and ideas. These interactions laid the foundation for the diffusion of Hindu traditions into African societies, leaving traces of cultural syncretism and shared heritage along the shores of the Indian Ocean.

Diaspora Communities:

The presence of Hinduism in Africa is also intricately linked to the migration of Indian laborers and merchants during the colonial era. In countries like Mauritius, Reunion Island, and South Africa, Indian diaspora communities brought with them their religious practices, rituals, and beliefs, contributing to the rich tapestry of cultural diversity in these regions. For example, in Mauritius, the vibrant Hindu community celebrates festivals like Diwali and Maha Shivaratri with great fervor, blending Indian traditions with local customs.

Cultural Syncretism:

The encounter between Hinduism and indigenous African religions has given rise to unique forms of syncretism and religious hybridity. In countries such as Kenya, Tanzania, and Madagascar, Hindu deities and rituals have been assimilated into the belief systems of local communities, resulting in fascinating blends of spirituality and cultural expression. The Swaminarayan Temple in Nairobi, Kenya, serves as a testament to this syncretic tradition, attracting devotees from diverse religious backgrounds.

Influence on Arts and Culture:

Hindu traditions have also left a profound imprint on the arts, music, and literature of African societies. In countries like South Africa and Mauritius, classical Indian dance forms such as Bharatanatyam and Kathak have found resonance among local performers and audiences, enriching the cultural landscape with their graceful movements and spiritual themes. Similarly, the influence of Hindu mythology and philosophy can be seen in African literature and poetry, where themes of karma, dharma, and liberation resonate with universal human experiences.

Community Institutions and Education:

Hindu temples and cultural centers serve as focal points for community cohesion, religious worship, and educational activities across Africa. In cities like Durban, Johannesburg, and Nairobi, temples provide a space for religious instruction, cultural preservation, and social networking among Hindu communities. Educational initiatives, such as Sunday schools and language classes, play a crucial role in transmitting Hindu values and teachings to future generations, ensuring the continuity of religious practices within African contexts.

Challenges and Opportunities:

Despite the vibrancy and resilience of Hindu traditions in the global African context, challenges such as religious pluralism, cultural assimilation, and social integration persist. Balancing the preservation of religious heritage with the imperative to adapt to local customs and values remains a constant endeavor for Hindu communities in Africa. Nevertheless, these challenges also present opportunities for dialogue, collaboration, and mutual understanding among diverse religious and cultural groups, fostering a spirit of inclusivity and harmony.

The presence of Hindu traditions in the global African context reflects the dynamic interplay between migration, cultural exchange, and religious adaptation. As Hindu communities continue to engage with African societies, their traditions and beliefs contribute to the rich mosaic of cultural diversity and spiritual expression on the continent. Through collective efforts to preserve and celebrate their religious heritage, Hindus in Africa affirm their identity, strengthen their bonds of solidarity, and contribute to the vibrant tapestry of multiculturalism in the African continent.

Chapter 13: Legacy of Language

Language stands as one of the most enduring and transformative legacies of our collective history. From ancient times to the present day, languages have served as vessels of culture, carriers of knowledge, and bridges of communication across diverse communities and civilizations. The Legacy of Language encapsulates the rich and multifaceted evolution of human communication, reflecting the ingenuity, creativity, and diversity of the human experience.

At its core, the Legacy of Language embodies the relentless quest of humanity to articulate thoughts, emotions, and experiences through spoken and written words. Language not only shapes our understanding of the world but also influences our perceptions, identities, and relationships with others. From the intricate scripts of ancient civilizations to the global lingua franca of the modern era, languages encapsulate the wisdom, traditions, and aspirations of countless generations, echoing through the corridors of time.

Through the lens of the Legacy of Language, we embark on a journey of exploration and discovery, unraveling the threads of linguistic diversity, language revitalization, and the interplay between language and identity. This exploration invites us to celebrate the richness and complexity of human expression, while also recognizing the challenges and opportunities inherent in the preservation, revitalization, and evolution of languages in an increasingly interconnected world. As we navigate the evolving landscape of language, we bear witness to the enduring legacy of linguistic heritage and the transformative power of words to shape our understanding of ourselves and the world around us.

Sanskrit's Global Footprint: Linguistic Links Across Continents

The study of languages reveals intricate connections that span continents, reflecting centuries of cultural exchange, migration, and trade. Linguistic links across continents highlight the shared origins, influences, and evolution of languages, underscoring the interconnectedness of human societies throughout history.

Indo-European Languages:

One of the most significant linguistic links across continents is the Indo-European language family, which encompasses languages spoken across Europe, South Asia, and parts of Central Asia. Sanskrit, the ancient language of India, shares linguistic roots with Latin and Greek, the classical languages of Europe. The similarities between Sanskrit, Latin, and Greek reveal the linguistic connections between ancient civilizations and highlight the shared Indo-European heritage.

Arabic Influence:

Arabic, a Semitic language originating in the Arabian Peninsula, has left a profound imprint on languages across Africa, the Middle East, and parts of Asia. Through trade routes and Islamic expansion, Arabic spread to regions as diverse as North Africa,

Spain, and the Indian subcontinent, influencing the vocabulary, grammar, and writing systems of local languages. For example, Swahili, a Bantu language spoken in East Africa, contains many loanwords of Arabic origin due to centuries of trade and cultural exchange along the Swahili coast.

Colonial Legacy:

The colonial era also left linguistic legacies that connect continents. European colonial powers, such as Portugal, Spain, Britain, and France, imposed their languages on territories they colonized, leading to the adoption of European languages as official or dominant languages in many regions of Africa, Asia, and the Americas. For instance, English serves as a lingua franca in former British colonies like India, Nigeria, and Singapore, while French is widely spoken in former French colonies in Africa.

Creole and Pidgin Languages:

Linguistic links across continents are also evident in creole and pidgin languages, which emerged through contact between speakers of different languages, often as a result of trade, colonization, or slavery. Creole languages such as Haitian Creole in the Caribbean and Tok Pisin in Papua New Guinea blend elements of European languages with African, indigenous, and other linguistic influences, creating vibrant new forms of communication that reflect the complex histories of their speakers.

Globalization and Hybrid Languages:

In the era of globalization, linguistic links across continents continue to evolve as languages intersect and hybridize in multicultural urban centers and online communities. Urban slang, youth vernaculars, and internet memes contribute to the emergence of hybrid languages and new forms of linguistic expression that transcend traditional boundaries. For example, Spanglish, a blend of Spanish and English spoken in the United States, reflects the cultural and linguistic fusion resulting from migration and cross-cultural interaction.

Linguistic links across continents serve as testament to the rich tapestry of human interaction, migration, and cultural exchange. From ancient trade routes to modern digital networks, languages connect people across vast distances, facilitating communication, understanding, and cooperation. As we explore the linguistic links that bind continents together, we gain insight into the shared heritage and interconnectedness of human societies, celebrating the diversity and resilience of language as a fundamental expression of human culture and identity.

Scriptural Translations: The Dissemination of Hindu Texts

The dissemination of Hindu texts through scriptural translations has played a pivotal role in spreading the wisdom, philosophy, and spiritual insights of Hinduism to diverse audiences across the globe. From ancient manuscripts to contemporary translations, the journey of Hindu scriptures transcends geographical and linguistic boundaries, enriching the lives of countless seekers and scholars worldwide.

Sanskrit Scriptures:

At the heart of Hinduism lie ancient texts written in Sanskrit, the sacred language of

Hindu tradition. The Vedas, Upanishads, Bhagavad Gita, and Puranas constitute the foundational scriptures of Hinduism, embodying profound philosophical insights, moral teachings, and spiritual guidance. Over the centuries, these scriptures have been meticulously preserved and transmitted through oral tradition and written manuscripts, forming the bedrock of Hindu religious and philosophical thought.

Regional Vernaculars:

The translation of Sanskrit scriptures into regional vernaculars has been instrumental in making Hindu texts accessible to wider audiences across India and beyond. From the Tamil translations of the Tirukkural to the Bengali renderings of the Ramayana and Mahabharata, regional languages have served as vehicles for transmitting Hindu wisdom to diverse linguistic communities. For example, the translations of the Bhagavad Gita into languages like Hindi, Tamil, Telugu, and Kannada have made its teachings accessible to millions of people across India and the Indian diaspora.

Global Reach:

In the era of globalization, the dissemination of Hindu texts has extended far beyond the Indian subcontinent, reaching audiences in every corner of the world. English translations of Hindu scriptures, scholarly commentaries, and popular interpretations have gained widespread popularity among Western audiences seeking spiritual guidance and philosophical insights. Works like Swami Vivekananda's "Complete Works" and Paramahansa Yogananda's "Autobiography of a Yogi" have introduced millions of readers to the timeless wisdom of Hindu philosophy.

Interfaith Dialogue:

The translation of Hindu scriptures has also facilitated interfaith dialogue and cross-cultural understanding, fostering exchanges between Hinduism and other religious traditions. Translations of Hindu texts into languages like Arabic, Chinese, and Spanish have sparked interest and dialogue among diverse religious communities, promoting mutual respect and appreciation for the spiritual heritage of different cultures. For example, the translation of the Bhagavad Gita into Arabic has contributed to interfaith discussions and scholarly exchanges in the Middle East.

Digital Platforms:

In the digital age, the dissemination of Hindu texts has been further accelerated through online platforms, e-books, and digital libraries. Websites and mobile applications offer a vast repository of Hindu scriptures, translations, and commentaries in multiple languages, making sacred texts accessible to a global audience with just a few clicks. Online forums and social media groups provide spaces for discussion, debate, and interpretation of Hindu scriptures, fostering a vibrant online community of seekers and scholars.

Scriptural translations have been instrumental in disseminating the wisdom and teachings of Hinduism to diverse audiences around the world. From ancient manuscripts to contemporary digital platforms, the journey of Hindu texts reflects the timeless quest for spiritual understanding and enlightenment. As translations continue to evolve and adapt to changing times, they serve as bridges of understanding, connecting people of different cultures and backgrounds through the shared wisdom of Hindu philosophy and spirituality.

Vernacular Variations: Hinduism's Influence on Local Languages

The influence of Hinduism on local languages, known as vernaculars, is profound and multifaceted, reflecting centuries of cultural exchange, religious dissemination, and literary expression. From the sacred hymns of the Vedas to the devotional poetry of saints and sages, Hinduism has enriched and shaped vernacular languages across the Indian subcontinent and beyond, leaving an indelible imprint on the linguistic landscape of diverse communities.

Regional Epics and Folklore:

One of the most significant manifestations of Hinduism's influence on local languages is found in regional epics and folklore. The Ramayana and Mahabharata, two ancient Indian epics, have been retold and reinterpreted in countless vernacular languages, including Tamil, Telugu, Bengali, and Kannada. These regional retellings not only preserve the essence of the original Sanskrit texts but also infuse them with local customs, traditions, and cultural motifs, making them accessible and relevant to diverse linguistic communities.

Devotional Literature:

Hinduism's influence on local languages is perhaps most pronounced in the realm of devotional literature. Bhakti poetry, composed by saint-poets across different regions of India, celebrates the divine through vernacular languages, offering heartfelt expressions of love, devotion, and surrender to the divine. The compositions of saints like Mirabai in Hindi, Purandara Dasa in Kannada, and Tulsidas in Awadhi exemplify the fusion of religious devotion with linguistic expression, inspiring generations of devotees and scholars alike.

Linguistic Syncretism:

Hinduism's influence on local languages has led to linguistic syncretism, where Sanskrit-derived vocabulary and idioms blend seamlessly with indigenous linguistic elements. For example, in Tamil Nadu, the classical Tamil language incorporates numerous Sanskrit loanwords related to religion, philosophy, and ritual practice, reflecting the enduring influence of Hinduism on Tamil culture and literature. Similarly, in Kerala, Malayalam literature is enriched by the incorporation of Sanskrit-derived terms and expressions, creating a unique linguistic tapestry that reflects the region's diverse religious and cultural heritage.

Cultural Expressions and Rituals:

The influence of Hinduism on local languages extends beyond literature to encompass cultural expressions, rituals, and everyday speech. Proverbs, idiomatic expressions, and ceremonial chants draw upon Hindu religious themes and symbols, imbuing vernacular languages with layers of meaning and significance. Rituals and festivals, conducted in regional languages, serve as vibrant expressions of community identity and religious devotion, reinforcing the enduring ties between Hinduism and local linguistic traditions.

Educational and Literary Revival:

In recent years, efforts to revive and promote regional languages have been intertwined with initiatives to preserve and disseminate Hindu cultural heritage. Educational institutions, literary societies, and cultural organizations play a crucial role in fostering linguistic pride and awareness among speakers of vernacular languages. Translation projects, aimed at making Hindu scriptures and philosophical texts accessible to vernacular audiences, contribute to the preservation and transmission of cultural knowledge across generations.

The influence of Hinduism on local languages reflects the dynamic interplay between religion, culture, and linguistic expression. Through regional epics, devotional literature, linguistic syncretism, cultural expressions, and educational initiatives, Hinduism has enriched and enlivened vernacular languages, shaping the linguistic identity and cultural heritage of diverse communities. As languages continue to evolve and adapt to changing social contexts, the legacy of Hinduism's influence on local languages serves as a testament to the enduring vitality and resilience of linguistic diversity in the Indian subcontinent and beyond.

Chapter 14: Artistic Alchemy

In the vast realm of human expression, an enchanting process unfolds—a process that transcends mere craftsmanship and delves into the depths of the soul. It's the phenomenon we term Artistic Alchemy, an intricate dance where raw materials, emotions, and visions converge to birth creations that stir the heart and spark the imagination.

At its core, Artistic Alchemy embodies the mystical transformation of the ordinary into the extraordinary, the mundane into the sublime. Across cultures, epochs, and mediums, artists harness the power of their creativity to distill emotions, experiences, and aspirations into tangible forms that resonate with audiences across generations.

From the ancient cave paintings that speak of humanity's earliest endeavors to communicate and connect, to the avant-garde installations that challenge our perceptions of reality, art serves as a timeless conduit for expression and exploration. It transcends linguistic barriers, cultural divides, and temporal constraints, inviting us to peer into the depths of our shared humanity and glimpse the essence of existence itself.

Through the lens of Artistic Alchemy, we embark on a journey of discovery—a journey that leads us through the labyrinthine corridors of creativity, where each brushstroke, each melody, each word holds the potential to unlock new dimensions of meaning and understanding. As we immerse ourselves in this enchanting realm, we bear witness to the alchemical process of creation, where the ordinary is transmuted into the extraordinary, and the artist becomes the conduit through which the mysteries of the universe find expression.

Temple Architecture: A Global Aesthetic Influence

Temple architecture stands as a testament to the ingenuity, spirituality, and artistic brilliance of civilizations across the globe. From the towering spires of Gothic cathedrals to the intricate carvings of Hindu temples, architectural marvels reflect the cultural and religious identities of societies throughout history. The influence of temple architecture extends far beyond religious boundaries, shaping the built environment and inspiring architectural styles across continents.

Hindu Temple Architecture:

In India, Hindu temple architecture showcases a diverse range of styles and techniques, from the towering vimanas of Dravidian temples in the south to the ornate shikharas of Nagara temples in the north. The Khajuraho temples, with their exquisite carvings depicting scenes from Hindu mythology, and the monumental Angkor Wat complex in Cambodia, are prime examples of the grandeur and intricacy of Hindu temple architecture.

Buddhist Stupas and Pagodas:

Buddhist architecture, particularly stupas

and pagodas, exhibits a harmonious blend of spiritual symbolism and architectural elegance. The ancient stupas of Sanchi in India, with their domed structures and elaborate gateways, exemplify the timeless appeal of Buddhist architectural principles. Similarly, the pagodas of East Asia, such as the Great Pagoda of Nara in Japan and the Shwedagon Pagoda in Myanmar, embody the serenity and grace of Buddhist aesthetics.

Islamic Influences:

Islamic architecture, characterized by intricate geometric patterns, calligraphy, and domed structures, has been profoundly influenced by temple architecture. The Mughal monuments of India, including the iconic Taj Mahal and the majestic Jama Masjid in Delhi, bear testament to the fusion of Islamic and Hindu architectural elements. The Alhambra in Spain, with its ornate courtyards and intricate tilework, reflects the enduring legacy of Islamic architectural traditions.

Classical Greek and Roman Temples:

Classical Greek and Roman temples, renowned for their Doric, Ionic, and Corinthian columns, have left an indelible mark on Western architectural styles. The Parthenon in Athens, dedicated to the goddess Athena, and the Pantheon in Rome, with its iconic dome and oculus, are iconic examples of classical temple architecture that continue to inspire architects and artists worldwide.

Gothic Cathedrals:

Gothic cathedrals, with their soaring spires, stained glass windows, and intricate stone carvings, represent the pinnacle of medieval European architecture. The Notre-Dame Cathedral in Paris and the Cologne Cathedral in Germany are celebrated examples of Gothic architecture, blending spiritual symbolism with artistic innovation to create awe-inspiring spaces of worship.

Temple architecture transcends geographical boundaries and cultural divides, serving as a testament to the universal human quest for spiritual expression and artistic excellence. Through its intricate designs, spiritual symbolism, and timeless beauty, temple architecture continues to inspire awe and admiration, shaping the built environment and cultural landscapes of civilizations across the globe. As we marvel at the architectural wonders of the past and present, we are reminded of the enduring legacy of temple architecture and its profound impact on the human experience.

Sculptural Traditions: Iconography and Symbolism in Hindu Art

Hindu art is a vibrant tapestry woven with intricate symbolism and profound spiritual significance. From the grand sculptures adorning temple walls to the delicate figurines found in household shrines, Hindu art reflects the rich tapestry of myth, legend, and religious belief that has evolved over millennia. At the heart of Hindu sculpture lies a complex system of iconography and symbolism that conveys deeper meanings and insights into the divine realms.

Iconography and Deity Representation:

Hindu sculpture abounds with representations of gods, goddesses, and divine beings, each with their own distinct iconography and symbolism. For example, Lord Shiva is often depicted with his trident, snake adornments, and third eye symbolizing destruction and regeneration. Goddess Lakshmi, the embodiment of wealth and prosperity, is depicted with lotus flowers and gold coins, symbolizing abundance and fortune.

Symbolism of Mudras and Postures:

Mudras, or hand gestures, play a significant role in Hindu sculpture, conveying specific meanings and intentions. The Abhaya mudra, or gesture of fearlessness, is commonly associated with Lord Buddha and signifies protection and reassurance. The Anjali mudra, a gesture of prayer and respect, is often depicted in depictions of gods and goddesses, symbolizing devotion and reverence.

Animal Symbolism and Sacred Beasts:

Animals hold a sacred place in Hindu mythology and are often depicted in sculptures as symbolic representations of divine qualities and attributes. The elephant-headed god Ganesha, remover of obstacles, is accompanied by his vahana, or vehicle, the mouse, symbolizing humility and resourcefulness. The bull, Nandi, serves as the mount of Lord Shiva and symbolizes strength, stability, and devotion.

Architectural Sculpture and Temple Art:

Hindu temples are adorned with intricate sculptures that narrate stories from mythology and depict celestial beings, mythical creatures, and divine symbols. The intricate carvings of the Khajuraho temples in Madhya Pradesh depict scenes of divine love and celestial dance, while the intricate reliefs of the Angkor Wat temple complex in Cambodia illustrate episodes from the Hindu epic, the Ramayana.

Regional Variations and Folk Art:

Hindu sculpture exhibits regional variations and folk art traditions that reflect local customs, beliefs, and cultural practices. The colorful terracotta figurines of Bankura in West Bengal depict scenes from rural life and mythology, while the bronze sculptures of Tamil Nadu showcase intricate details and craftsmanship.

Hindu sculpture is a visual feast of symbolism, iconography, and artistic expression that reflects the diverse tapestry of Hindu mythology, spirituality, and cultural heritage. Through its intricate carvings, divine figures, and sacred motifs, Hindu art invites viewers to explore the depths of the human spirit and contemplate the mysteries of existence. As we marvel at the beauty and complexity of Hindu sculpture, we are reminded of the enduring legacy of artistic expression and spiritual wisdom that continues to inspire and uplift humanity across generations.

Manuscript Illumination: Preserving Hindu Knowledge in Illustrated Form

Manuscript illumination stands as a timeless art form that has played a pivotal role in preserving and transmitting Hindu knowledge and wisdom through the ages. Illuminated manuscripts, adorned with

intricate illustrations and vibrant colors,
serve as repositories of Hindu scriptures,
epics, and philosophical treatises, enriching
our understanding of Hindu culture,
spirituality, and artistic expression.

Ancient Manuscript Traditions:

The tradition of manuscript illumination in
Hinduism dates back to ancient times when
scribes meticulously transcribed sacred
texts onto palm leaves, birch bark, or
parchment. These manuscripts were
embellished with ornate calligraphy,
elaborate borders, and exquisite
illustrations depicting scenes from Hindu
mythology, cosmology, and religious rituals.
The Bower Manuscript, discovered in
Kashmir, is one such example, containing
illustrations of deities, celestial beings, and
mythical creatures.

Illuminated Manuscripts of the Bhagavad Gita:

The Bhagavad Gita, a revered scripture of Hinduism, has been illuminated in countless manuscripts across different regions and time periods. These illuminated manuscripts often feature miniature paintings depicting the dialogue between Lord Krishna and Prince Arjuna on the battlefield of Kurukshetra. The Srimad Bhagavad Gita manuscript from 18th-century Bengal is renowned for its exquisite illustrations of Krishna's divine form and the cosmic vision revealed to Arjuna.

Ramayana and Mahabharata Manuscripts:

The Ramayana and Mahabharata, two epic narratives of Hindu mythology, have been illuminated in numerous manuscripts, each reflecting regional styles and artistic interpretations. The Mewar Ramayana, created in the 17th century under the patronage of Maharana Jagat Singh of Mewar, is celebrated for its intricate illustrations depicting the epic deeds of Lord Rama and his companions. Similarly, the Razmnama, a Persian translation of the Mahabharata, contains vibrant illustrations of the epic's key events and characters.

Jain Manuscript Illumination:

Jainism, a religious tradition closely related to Hinduism, also boasts a rich tradition of manuscript illumination. Jain manuscripts, known as palm leaf manuscripts or pothi, are adorned with intricate paintings depicting scenes from Jain mythology, the lives of Tirthankaras, and the principles of Jain philosophy. The Kalpasutra manuscript, created in Gujarat during the 15th century, is renowned for its exquisite illustrations of Jain cosmology and religious narratives.

Contemporary Revival and Conservation Efforts:

In recent years, there has been a renewed interest in the art of manuscript illumination, fueled by efforts to preserve and document traditional knowledge systems. Artisans and scholars collaborate to digitize ancient manuscripts, conserve fragile artworks, and revive traditional techniques of manuscript illumination. Initiatives such as the Digital Library of India and the National Mission for Manuscripts aim to digitize and catalog manuscripts, making them accessible to scholars and enthusiasts worldwide.

Manuscript illumination serves as a timeless testament to the ingenuity, creativity, and spiritual devotion of Hindu artisans and scribes. Through intricate illustrations, vibrant colors, and meticulous craftsmanship, illuminated manuscripts preserve and transmit Hindu knowledge and wisdom across generations, enriching our understanding of Hindu culture, mythology, and spirituality. As custodians of this rich heritage, we honor the legacy of manuscript illumination and celebrate its enduring contribution to the tapestry of human civilization.

Chapter 15: Modern Reverberations

In the maze of contemporary existence, echoes of ancient wisdom linger, weaving through the tapestry of modern thought and molding the collective ethos of humanity. This exploration delves into the enduring resonance of age-old traditions, philosophies, and cultural paradigms in today's dynamic and fast-evolving world. From the realms of spiritual sanctuaries to the arenas of intellectual discourse, traces of the past intertwine with the innovations of the present, offering profound insights into the human experience and avenues for transcendence.

In an epoch characterized by globalization

and technological prowess, the quest for significance and authenticity endures as an intrinsic pursuit of the human psyche. This narrative seeks to unravel the intricate threads that bind ancient wisdom to contemporary challenges, elucidating how time-honored philosophies continue to shape our perceptions of morality, ethics, and existential inquiries. Through a kaleidoscope of cultural perspectives and interdisciplinary discourse, this journey explores the nuanced ways in which ancient traditions reverberate in the context of modernity, permeating realms of art, literature, science, and spirituality.

As we navigate the complexities of contemporary life, this narrative beckons us to pause, reflect, and engage with the timeless legacies of antiquity. Through dialogue, introspection, and creative expression, we embark on a voyage of exploration—a journey that transcends temporal confines and illuminates the perennial truths that animate our shared human journey.

Hinduism Today: Contemporary Expressions Beyond India

In the contemporary world, Hinduism continues to evolve and manifest itself in diverse expressions beyond the borders of India. As globalization, migration, and cultural exchange redefine societal landscapes, the influence of Hinduism extends far and wide, shaping beliefs, practices, and identities in various corners of the globe.

Diaspora Communities:

Hindu diaspora communities scattered across North America, Europe, Australia, and beyond have become vibrant hubs of Hindu practice and cultural expression. Temples, community centers, and cultural organizations serve as focal points for religious observances, social gatherings, and educational initiatives. For instance, the Hindu American Foundation in the United States promotes Hindu advocacy and education, while the Hindu Council of Australia fosters interfaith dialogue and community engagement.

Fusion of Tradition and Modernity:

In contemporary Hinduism, traditional practices seamlessly blend with modern adaptations to meet the needs of the present-day world. From yoga studios in New York City to vegetarian restaurants in

London, Hindu-inspired lifestyles resonate with individuals seeking spiritual fulfillment, holistic well-being, and ethical living. The International Society for Krishna Consciousness (ISKCON), founded in New York in 1966, has established temples, schools, and outreach programs worldwide, promoting the teachings of Bhagavad Gita in modern contexts.

Digital and Social Media:

The digital age has ushered in new avenues for the dissemination of Hindu teachings and practices. Websites, blogs, podcasts, and social media platforms serve as virtual forums for dialogue, debate, and community building. Channels like Sadhguru's YouTube channel and Amma's social media presence attract millions of followers worldwide, offering spiritual guidance, inspirational messages, and live events accessible to global audiences.

Cultural Festivals and Celebrations:

Hindu festivals and celebrations have transcended cultural boundaries, becoming popular events celebrated worldwide. Diwali, the Festival of Lights, illuminates cities from London to Singapore with colorful lights, fireworks, and cultural performances. Navratri, the nine-night festival honoring the divine feminine, sees spirited dance gatherings in cities across North America, Europe, and beyond.

Interfaith Dialogue and Engagement:

Hinduism today actively participates in interfaith dialogue and engagement, fostering understanding, cooperation, and harmony among diverse religious communities. Organizations like the

Parliament of the World's Religions bring together leaders and practitioners from various faith traditions to discuss shared values, social justice issues, and environmental sustainability.

Environmental Stewardship and Social Justice:

Drawing inspiration from Hindu teachings of dharma (duty) and ahimsa (non-violence), contemporary Hindu movements advocate for environmental stewardship, animal welfare, and social justice. Projects like the Hare Krishna Food for Life initiative provide vegetarian meals to millions of people in need worldwide, embodying the principle of seva (selfless service) in action.

Hinduism today exhibits dynamic expressions beyond India's borders, reflecting the adaptability, resilience, and universality of its teachings and practices. Through diaspora communities, fusion of tradition and modernity, digital outreach, cultural festivals, interfaith dialogue, and social activism, Hinduism continues to thrive and evolve, enriching the global tapestry of religious and cultural diversity.

Cultural Heritage Conservation: Preserving Global Hindu Monuments

The conservation of Hindu monuments worldwide is a vital endeavor aimed at safeguarding the rich cultural heritage and architectural marvels that bear testament to the ingenuity and spiritual legacy of Hindu civilization. From ancient temples to sacred sites, these monuments serve as repositories of history, art, and religious tradition, embodying the aspirations and achievements of generations past.

Angkor Wat, Cambodia:

Angkor Wat stands as a magnificent testament to Hindu-Buddhist art and architecture in Southeast Asia. Constructed in the 12th century during the Khmer Empire, this UNESCO World Heritage Site features intricate carvings depicting Hindu deities and epic narratives such as the Ramayana and Mahabharata. Conservation efforts led by the Cambodian government and international organizations aim to preserve Angkor Wat's structural integrity and cultural significance for future generations.

Prambanan Temple, Indonesia:

Located on the island of Java, the Prambanan Temple complex is a masterpiece of Hindu architecture dedicated to the Trimurti—Brahma, Vishnu, and Shiva. Dating back to the 9th century, this UNESCO World Heritage Site comprises towering stone structures adorned with intricate reliefs depicting scenes from Hindu mythology. Conservation initiatives supported by the Indonesian government and heritage organizations focus on structural stabilization, restoration of stone carvings, and environmental management to mitigate threats from pollution and natural disasters.

Brihadeeswarar Temple, India:

The Brihadeeswarar Temple, also known as the Big Temple, is a towering marvel of Dravidian architecture located in Thanjavur, Tamil Nadu. Built by the Chola king Rajaraja I in the 11th century, this UNESCO World Heritage Site features a colossal Shiva lingam and intricately carved gopurams (gateway towers). Ongoing conservation efforts by the Archaeological Survey of India include structural repairs, documentation of architectural features, and environmental monitoring to ensure the longevity of this architectural treasure.

Pashupatinath Temple, Nepal:

Situated on the banks of the Bagmati River in Kathmandu, the Pashupatinath Temple is one of the holiest shrines in Hinduism dedicated to Lord Shiva. Dating back to the 5th century, this UNESCO World Heritage Site attracts pilgrims and devotees from around the world. Conservation projects led by the Pashupati Area Development Trust focus on heritage preservation, temple restoration, and environmental conservation along the sacred riverbanks.

BAPS Shri Swaminarayan Mandir, United

Kingdom:

The BAPS Shri Swaminarayan Mandir in London stands as a stunning example of traditional Hindu temple architecture outside of India. Constructed using ancient Vedic principles and craftsmanship, this marble masterpiece serves as a center for worship, cultural education, and community engagement. Conservation efforts by the Bochasanwasi Akshar Purushottam Swaminarayan Sanstha (BAPS) emphasize maintenance, repair, and restoration to ensure the Mandir's architectural integrity and spiritual significance.

The conservation of global Hindu monuments is essential for preserving the cultural heritage, artistic legacy, and spiritual significance of these sacred sites. Through collaborative efforts between governments, heritage organizations, and local communities, these monuments serve as living testaments to the enduring legacy of Hindu civilization, inspiring awe and reverence for generations to come.

Interfaith Dialogues: Hindu Contributions to Global Spiritual Discourse

Interfaith dialogues play a crucial role in fostering understanding, cooperation, and mutual respect among diverse religious traditions worldwide. Hinduism, with its rich philosophical heritage and inclusive ethos, has made significant contributions to global spiritual discourse through interfaith engagement, dialogue, and collaboration.

Parliament of the World's Religions:

The Parliament of the World's Religions, founded in 1893, serves as a prominent platform for interfaith dialogue and collaboration. Hindu delegates and spiritual leaders participate in this global assembly to discuss shared values, promote social justice, and address pressing issues facing humanity. The Parliament provides opportunities for Hindu representatives to engage with leaders from other faith traditions, fostering understanding and cooperation on matters of mutual concern.

Swami Vivekananda's Address in Chicago:

Swami Vivekananda's historic address at the Parliament of the World's Religions in Chicago in 1893 is a landmark moment in the history of interfaith dialogue. His eloquent speech on the universality of religions and the harmony of faiths resonated with audiences worldwide, emphasizing the inclusive nature of Hindu philosophy and its relevance in addressing contemporary challenges. Vivekananda's message of tolerance, acceptance, and spiritual unity continues to inspire interfaith efforts to this day.

Hindu-Jewish Dialogue:

Interfaith dialogues between Hindu and Jewish communities have deepened understanding and collaboration between two ancient traditions. Shared values of ethical living, social justice, and respect for diversity form the basis of mutual engagement. Initiatives such as the Hindu-Jewish Leadership Summit facilitate dialogue, exchange, and cooperation on issues of common interest, fostering relationships of trust and friendship.

Yoga and Mindfulness Practices:

Hindu contributions to global spiritual discourse extend beyond formal dialogues to the widespread adoption of yoga, meditation, and mindfulness practices. These ancient techniques, rooted in Hindu philosophy and spirituality, have gained popularity worldwide for their therapeutic benefits and holistic approach to well-being. Yoga studios, meditation centers, and wellness retreats serve as spaces for interfaith dialogue, where individuals from diverse backgrounds come together to explore shared spiritual experiences and insights.

Environmental Stewardship and Social Justice:

Hindu teachings on environmental stewardship, non-violence, and social justice contribute to global conversations

on sustainability and human rights.
Organizations like the Bhumi Project and
the International Society for Krishna
Consciousness (ISKCON) advocate for
ecological preservation, vegetarianism, and
humanitarian aid, engaging with diverse
faith communities and secular organizations
to address pressing global challenges.

Hindu contributions to interfaith dialogues
enrich global spiritual discourse by
promoting principles of tolerance,
compassion, and unity in diversity. Through
dialogue, collaboration, and shared action,
Hindus and adherents of other faith
traditions work together to build bridges of
understanding, promote peace, and create
a more harmonious world.

Reflections

In our odyssey through the annals of history, we've traced Hinduism's profound influence beyond India's borders, unveiling its timeless wisdom across diverse landscapes. As we conclude this journey, it's a moment of reflection—a pause to contemplate the insights gleaned from our exploration.

From the ancient civilizations of the Indus Valley to the distant shores of Southeast Asia and the Pacific Islands, Hinduism's presence has left an indelible mark. Through temples, monuments, and philosophical discourse, we've witnessed the resilience and adaptability of this ancient tradition.

Interfaith dialogues, cultural exchanges, and diaspora communities have further enriched Hinduism's global footprint, inspiring seekers and scholars alike. As we bid farewell, let's carry forward the lessons learned and the connections forged, embracing the unity in diversity that Hinduism embodies.

This journey isn't just a scholarly pursuit—it's a spiritual odyssey, a quest for understanding and harmony. As we contemplate the intersections of faith and culture, let's honor Hinduism's legacy and celebrate its contributions to humanity. In the tapestry of existence, let's embrace the timeless truths that unite us all.

The Living Tapestry: Reflections on Hinduism's Global Journey

As we reflect on Hinduism's global journey, we witness a living tapestry woven with threads of spirituality, culture, and tradition that transcend geographical boundaries. Through diverse landscapes and cultural contexts, Hinduism has evolved and adapted, leaving an indelible mark on the collective consciousness of humanity.

Temples as Sacred Spaces:

Throughout the world, Hindu temples stand as sacred spaces where devotees gather to worship, reflect, and seek spiritual solace. Examples include the BAPS Shri Swaminarayan Mandir in London, the Murugan Temple in Malaysia, and the Sri Venkateswara Temple in the United States.

These temples serve as vibrant centers of community life, fostering cultural exchange and spiritual growth.

Festivals and Rituals:

Hindu festivals such as Diwali, Holi, and Navratri resonate far beyond the borders of India, uniting communities in celebration and reverence. In countries like Mauritius, Fiji, and Trinidad and Tobago, these festivals are celebrated with fervor, blending Hindu traditions with local customs and traditions. The vibrant colors, music, and rituals reflect the diversity and richness of Hindu cultural heritage.

Yoga and Mindfulness:

The practice of yoga and mindfulness has transcended cultural barriers, becoming a global phenomenon embraced by people of all backgrounds. From the bustling streets of New York City to the serene landscapes of Bali, yoga studios and wellness retreats offer seekers a pathway to physical health, mental well-being, and spiritual growth. The ancient teachings of yoga, rooted in Hindu philosophy, continue to inspire millions worldwide.

Interfaith Dialogue and Collaboration:

Hinduism's message of inclusivity and tolerance has fostered interfaith dialogue and collaboration on a global scale. Initiatives such as the Parliament of the World's Religions and the Hindu-Jewish Leadership Summit bring together religious leaders, scholars, and activists to promote understanding, peace, and cooperation. Through dialogue and mutual respect, Hindus engage with people of diverse faith traditions to address shared challenges and pursue common goals.

Cultural Preservation and Revival:

In regions such as Bali, Nepal, and Sri Lanka, efforts are underway to preserve and revitalize Hindu cultural heritage. Traditional arts, music, dance, and literature are celebrated and nurtured, ensuring that future generations inherit a rich tapestry of cultural expression. Festivals, rituals, and ceremonies serve as reminders of the enduring legacy of Hinduism and its contributions to global civilization.

Hinduism's global journey is a testament to its resilience, adaptability, and enduring relevance in an ever-changing world. As we navigate the complexities of modern life, the timeless teachings of Hinduism continue to inspire and guide us, weaving a tapestry of unity, diversity, and spiritual awakening for all humanity.

Unfinished Narratives: Inviting Further Exploration and Research

Within the expansive tapestry of Hinduism's global journey, there exist countless threads of exploration, discovery, and inquiry awaiting further unraveling. These unfinished narratives beckon scholars, researchers, and seekers to delve deeper into the complexities and nuances of Hinduism's multifaceted presence across the world.

Archaeological Discoveries:

Numerous archaeological sites across Asia,

Africa, Europe, and the Pacific Islands hold untold stories of Hinduism's historical footprint. From the ruins of ancient temples in Cambodia's Angkor Wat to submerged relics off the coast of Indonesia, each discovery offers tantalizing glimpses into the past, prompting questions about trade networks, cultural exchanges, and religious syncretism.

Diaspora Communities:

The experiences of Hindu diaspora communities in countries like the United States, Canada, and the United Kingdom present rich avenues for exploration. From the formation of vibrant cultural associations to the adaptation of religious practices in new environments, these communities offer insights into questions of identity, belonging, and cultural continuity.

Linguistic and Literary Traditions:

The study of Sanskrit literature, regional languages, and vernacular texts provides fertile ground for further research. From ancient epics like the Mahabharata and Ramayana to classical treatises on philosophy, ethics, and aesthetics, Hindu literary traditions offer a treasure trove of wisdom waiting to be unearthed and analyzed.

Cultural Syncretism and Hybridity:

In regions where Hinduism intersected with other religious and cultural traditions, such as Southeast Asia, East Africa, and the Caribbean, the dynamics of cultural syncretism and hybridity invite nuanced exploration. How did Hindu beliefs and practices interact with local customs, beliefs, and worldviews? What forms of cultural adaptation and integration emerged from these encounters?

Contemporary Challenges and Transformations:

The challenges and transformations facing Hinduism in the modern world present pressing areas for inquiry. From debates over caste, gender, and social justice to the impact of globalization, technology, and secularism, the evolving landscape of Hinduism demands critical engagement and analysis.

As scholars and researchers embark on these journeys of exploration, they contribute to a deeper understanding of Hinduism's global impact and significance. By unraveling the unfinished narratives embedded within its history, culture, and spirituality, they illuminate new pathways of inquiry, dialogue, and discovery for generations to come. In the pursuit of knowledge and understanding, the narratives of Hinduism continue to evolve, inviting us all to participate in the ongoing dialogue of human civilization.

Epilogue: Hinduism's Timeless Echoes in the Contemporary World

In this epilogue, we reflect on the enduring resonance of Hinduism's teachings and traditions in the ever-evolving landscape of the contemporary world. From its ancient roots to its modern manifestations, Hinduism's timeless echoes continue to shape and inspire individuals, communities, and societies around the globe.

Spiritual Seekers and Yogic Wisdom:

In today's fast-paced world, the quest for inner peace, mindfulness, and spiritual fulfillment has led many to explore the teachings of Hinduism, particularly through the practice of yoga and meditation. Yoga studios, retreat centers, and wellness programs offer spaces for individuals to reconnect with themselves and cultivate holistic well-being. The ancient wisdom of the Bhagavad Gita, the Upanishads, and other Hindu texts resonates deeply with those seeking spiritual guidance in the midst of modern challenges.

Cultural Diversity and Pluralism:

Hinduism's emphasis on diversity, tolerance, and pluralism serves as a beacon of inspiration in an increasingly interconnected world. In multicultural societies, festivals such as Diwali, Holi, and Navratri are celebrated with enthusiasm and joy, fostering a spirit of inclusivity and mutual respect. Hindu values of ahimsa (non-violence), seva (selfless service), and dharma (righteous duty) provide ethical frameworks for addressing contemporary social, environmental, and political issues.

Environmental Stewardship and Sustainability:

Hinduism's reverence for nature and the interconnectedness of all life has inspired movements for environmental stewardship and sustainability. From eco-friendly practices in Hindu temples to initiatives promoting vegetarianism and animal welfare, Hindus worldwide are increasingly recognizing their responsibility to protect and preserve the natural world. The principles of vasudhaiva kutumbakam (the world is one family) and karma yoga (selfless action) guide efforts to promote ecological balance and harmony.

Social Justice and Humanitarianism:

Hinduism's emphasis on social justice, compassion, and service to others inspires a multitude of humanitarian initiatives and charitable endeavors. Organizations such as Akshaya Patra, the Art of Living Foundation, and Chinmaya Mission work tirelessly to alleviate poverty, promote education, and provide healthcare to underserved communities. The spirit of seva (selfless service) and karuna (compassion) animates efforts to address the root causes of suffering and inequality in society.

Interfaith Dialogue and Global Citizenship:

In an increasingly diverse and interconnected world, Hinduism's teachings on interfaith harmony, respect for diversity, and global citizenship resonate deeply with individuals and communities of all backgrounds. Interfaith dialogue initiatives, such as the Hindu-Muslim Unity Forum and the Parliament of the World's Religions, foster mutual understanding, cooperation, and solidarity among people of different faith traditions. By embracing the principles of sarva dharma samabhava (equal respect for all religions) and vasudhaiva kutumbakam (the world is one family), Hindus contribute to building bridges of peace and understanding in a divided world.

As we contemplate the timeless echoes of Hinduism in the contemporary world, we are reminded of its profound capacity to inspire, uplift, and transform lives. In the face of modern challenges and uncertainties, the timeless wisdom of Hinduism offers guidance, solace, and hope for a brighter future for all humanity.

www.ingramcontent.com/pod-product-compliance
Lightning Source LLC
Chambersburg PA
CBHW060518160726
47991CB00001B/84